DOWN THE LINE TO DOVER

£3

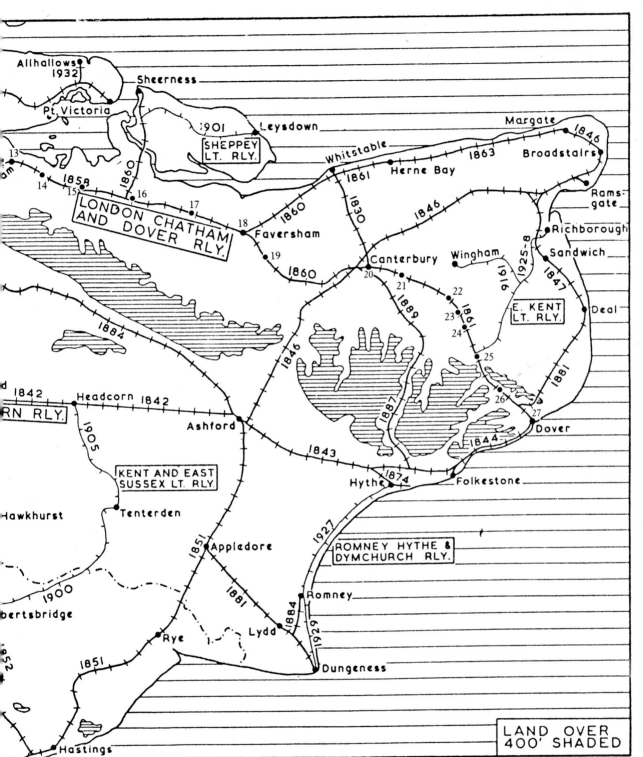

Allhallows
1932
Pt. Victoria
Sheerness
13
1858
14
15
16
1860
17
18
Faversham
LONDON CHATHAM
AND DOVER RLY.
19
1860
1901
Leysdown
SHEPPEY
LT. RLY.
Whitstable
1861
1830
1860
Herne Bay
1846
Margate
1846
1863
Broadstairs
Rams-gate
Richborough
Wingham
Canterbury
20
21
1889
1846
22
23
24
1861
1916
1925-8
1847
Sandwich
E. KENT
LT. RLY.
Deal
25
1881
1842
Headcorn 1842
RN RLY.
1905
Ashford
1884
26
27
Dover
1887
1843
1844
Hythe
1874
Folkestone
KENT AND EAST
SUSSEX LT. RLY.
Hawkhurst
Tenterden
1851
Appledore
1927
ROMNEY HYTHE &
DYMCHURCH RLY.
1900
1881
bertsbridge
Rye
Lydd
1884
Romney
1929
Dungeness
1952
1851
Hastings

LAND OVER
400' SHADED

DOWN THE LINE TO DOVER

A pictorial history of Kent's boat train line

MURIEL V. SEARLE

MIDAS BOOKS

Dedicated to my aunt,
Mary Irene (Renie) Searle

In the same illustrated series:

Metro Memories by Dennis Edwards and Ron Pigram
Romance of Metro-Land by Dennis Edwards and Ron Pigram
The Golden Years of the Metropolitan Railway by Dennis Edwards and Ron Pigram
The Routemaster Bus by Colin Curtis
The Final Link by Dennis Edwards and Ron Pigram
Midland Line Memories by Brian Radford
London's Underground Stations by Laurence Menear

General Editor: Brian Jewell

First published in 1983 by
MIDAS BOOKS
12 Dene Way, Speldhurst
Tunbridge Wells, Kent TN3 0NX

© Muriel V. Searle 1983

ISBN 0 85936 206 X

Printed in Great Britain by
Chambers Green Ltd,
Tunbridge Wells, Kent

Contents

Acknowledgements

The author has many people to thank for help during the compilation of this book, in particular:

Mr Philip Tyrrell, Mr S.R.W. Anderson, Dr P. Ransome Wallis, the Rev. C. Stone, Mr A.G. Stone, Mr J. Chinery, Mr S. Gower, Mr M.E. Joyce, Adams & Dart Ltd (Thorne's *Environs of London*), Home Words Publishing Co. Ltd, Ward Lock Ltd (old railway advertisements), Methuen London Ltd (H.V. Morton's *London*), Kentish Times Newspapers Ltd (Hop specials), Sea Containers (SeaCo Group), Venice Simplon-Orient-Express Ltd with Mr Alan Pegler, Manston Preservation Group, *The Times* (accident at Beckenham 1866). An extract from Cassell's *Book of Knowledge* appears by permission of Collier Macmillan Ltd.

Cartoons are reproduced by permission of *Punch*; other drawings and engravings come from Home Words Publishing Co. Ltd. Pictures other than those in the author's collection were kindly loaned by Lens of Sutton; Dr P. Ransome Wallis; Mr Philip Tyrrell; Sea Containers; Venice Simplon-Orient-Express Ltd.

Any owners of *The Cray* and the *Bromley Record* (ceased publication in 1873 and 1913 respectively) have proved impossible to trace after a minimum of seventy years. It is hoped that this very sincere acknowledgement will be accepted.

The help of Bromley Public Library, Local Studies Department, is also gratefully acknowledged.

Introduction

The main line from Victoria to Dover, on British Rail's Southern Region, has almost from its earliest days possessed a certain air of distinction – even glamour – born of its function as one of the two rail-borne Continental gateways of Kent.

Yet this interesting line grew from such inconsiderable beginnings as the little Mid-Kent Railway, and was finally put together against a background of perpetual antagonism between the two arch-rivals of Kent: the South Eastern, and the London, Chatham & Dover railways. The South Eastern's own route to Dover, via its twin port of Folkestone, pre-dated the LCDR by some years.

The Victoria – Bromley – Chatham – Faversham – Canterbury – Dover main-line route of today is unusual in that its building began halfway across Kent and thence probed still farther away from the capital, only at a later date reaching backwards towards London.

Such a route inevitably drew to itself a store of background fact, lore and even fiction, now given a certain nostalgia by the fact that of all of its once-famous trains only one still exists, and that as a revival rather than an original.

Even so, this is still one of England's busiest lines to any port, though with the one superb exception the many daily departures for Dover and Folkestone docks run unnamed and unsung; mere figures on a working timetable. At the same time, the Londonward part of the network provides one of Britain's most intensive daily commuter services, and the whole line continues to support a very busy freight business in almost every commodity from tomatoes and onions to tractors, or coal from the Kent colliery.

For the sake of completeness, though considering primarily this ex-LCDR route via Chatham, we include those boat trains which either regularly or sporadically also used the more southerly former SER line via Folkestone into Dover, on the grounds that they followed our own line for a lengthy section of their journeys (about thirteen miles, or nearly 20 per cent of the way) before turning off through Orpington to finish their run via the alternative Channel port of Folkestone. Among them was the *Golden Arrow*, without which no book about railways to Dover would be complete.

1
Railway Mania

'This road does not appear to be much used; neither is it probable that it will *ever* come into general use; the expense attending the formation of [railways] is enormous, and the advantages, and consequently the gain, are confined to carriage in only one direction.' So concluded a particularly short-sighted observer of the Grand Surrey Iron Rail Way in 1811, within riding distance of the area that would soon support the first public railway south of Liverpool.

Within less than two decades he was triumphantly proved wrong, when the pioneer Canterbury & Whitstable Railway brought steam-powered railed locomotion to Kent in 1830, long before London saw a train.

Coincidentally, the C&WR came into the same area that subsequently became the Boat Train Line, the 'Land 'em Smash 'em and Over', or in polite public parlance simply The Chatham.

The Canterbury & Whitstable Railway opened on 3 May 1830. Only a few years later it scored another 'first' by issuing Britain's first railway season tickets, thus creating the railway commuter.

Almost at right angles to the C&WR line, about two decades onwards, evolved the more important artery that is now the main Victoria – Dover line, coming within a mile of the C&W terminus at Canterbury without actually touching it.

Dover's first railways

Between these two phases of development Dover endured or perhaps enjoyed its last railwayless years, not only as a port but also as a resort for wealthy invalids.

By about 1840 the growth of Dover had become more rapid and more noticeable to outsiders. Fine new houses were being built on the Marine Parade by hopeful speculative builders. Liverpool Terrace was under construction, and the first houses were appearing under the steep Castle cliff; on the flatter ground, west of the castle by the seafront, were new public baths. The housing boom closed in from all sides, turning a small port into a residential town; many of the new properties were in an aristocratic price bracket, as the day of the seaside watering place brought fashion as well as commerce into Dover, for genteel summer dalliance or for seasonal winter residence.

15

Even before trains, cross-Channel day trips were provided by packet-boat, but for the rich rather than for Everyman. These wealthy travellers had a different reason for going across – not tourism but health. The Channel was reckoned to be therapeutic, and some invalids deliberately sought a bout of *mal de mer* as part of their internal cleansing. Here a doctor writes in 1841: 'To the bilious, instead of taking constant medicines, I recommend embarking, when the day is fine, on board a sailing packet or steamer and cross over to Calais or Boulogne in hopes of being made seasick. This operation empties the stomach more effectually than can be done by means of emetics. . . . This plan may be adopted twice or three times in the course of a two or three months' residence.'

The South Eastern Railway, the Chatham's arch-rival, was first into Dover with the south-easterly route via Folkestone which is still in use, and thence along the narrow ledge between the beach and the Warren into Dover; this line opened on 7 February 1844. In 1843 the SER had negotiated an agreement with the New Commercial Steam Packet Company to open up the crossing to Boulogne to railways, paving the way to Kent's supremacy as a boat-train route and looking prophetically forward to the modern BR-Sealink concept.

In 1844 the SER was able to establish a combined rail–sea venture by forming the South Eastern & Continental Steam Packet Company, serving Calais and Boulogne and also Ostend in Belgium. In January 1849 came its newest Continental connection, an extension from Folkestone town down to the harbour itself.

Kentishmen quickly realized that the time was ripe for a more direct approach to the Kent ports from the county's interior and such important towns as Chatham, Rochester and Canterbury, with Dover as the main objective.

As the 1850s opened it was obvious that Dover deserved a better service than the SER could offer, for its vital statistics were already impressive: a Parliamentary Borough and ancient Cinque Port with a market trade of its own, it elected two Members to Parliament, and its corporation revenue was slightly in excess of £5000. Over a hundred ships were registered there.

Though still a difficult approach because of shifting shingle banks, the harbour was in the throes of considerable improvements. It included three dock basins, the principal one sheltered by two piers, and the steam-packet service across to France and Belgium was greatly prospering, while in return those countries sent to Dover supplies of dairy foods, fruit and vegetables.

Agitation mounted in north and central Kent for a railway running more directly, in a straight line down to Faversham and thence in another straight line into Dover; an almost unassailable challenge to the already existing SER. So began the geographically curious construction of the Victoria to Dover line, in two quite

Driving in the rain; the spirit that made the 'Land 'em Smash 'em and Over' in its earliest days.

Invicta, the first railway locomotive south of Liverpool, used on the Canterbury & Whitstable Railway of 1830. For many years *Invicta* served as a reminder to the people of Canterbury of the illustrious past by standing on an outside site. Since this 1979 photograph, *Invicta* has been moved indoors.

separate sections; firstly, from a point halfway across the county and onwards to the port, starting at the Medway towns; secondly, from west to east again, ultimately joining London and the Medway. The latter was destined, like many another main line, to open erratically in short sections under several minor companies.

The longest of these two phases, from Chatham and Rochester to Dover, opened in stages between 1858 and 1861. In 1850 a company had been formed by T.R. Crampton, engineer, a Mr Morris, Lord Harris, and George Burns, contractor. Its composition soon changed into a ruling bevy led by Crampton alone, with other new gentleman backers. On 25 January 1858 their line was opened between Chatham and Faversham, past Gillingham and Sittingbourne, a substantial part of the ultimate main line and well on the way to Dover. A few weeks later work was completed on the first leg working backwards towards London, an extension of one station to Rochester (Strood), opening on 29 March. It was already possible to travel from Rochester to Faversham in a mere fifty minutes; slow by today's standard of a twenty-minute ride, but a huge improvement on the horse.

In July 1860, Sheerness to the north acquired a branch from Sittingbourne; Sheerness was then a major naval base, and neighbouring Queenborough was a flourishing port for Holland

Massive ruins of earlier railway architecture at the eastern end of Rochester Bridge, seen from a train on the present tracks.

and northern Europe – a boat-train objective in itself.

The East Kent Railway had begun back in 1853, being intended to consolidate a through London – Chatham run. Financially, however, it was so precarious that the South Eastern could not take seriously its threat to the SER territory. Nor did it bother to take up the EKR's offer to lease or sell its property to the older company in 1855. Instead it let the EKR plod on, routing its traffic over SER tracks – at a price.

In 1859 the time had come for forging ahead again, changing the title of East Kent Railway to the more geographically accurate one of London, Chatham & Dover. Nevertheless, the names East Kent and Mid Kent still continued in everyday usage and on timetables.

In July 1860 track was opened east of Faversham to Canterbury, completing the first leg of the first (eastern) section.

Dover is reached

From 22 July 1861 the East Kent's initial stage was almost complete, when it finally reached Dover Town (now Dover Priory). Only one short length here remained for completion, down to the main goal of Dover Harbour – later renamed Dover Marine, and renamed again in about 1980 as Dover Western Docks, or DWD in railway parlance.

18

Where the Canterbury & Whitstable Railway was carried across the later Kent Coast main line, which leaves the Dover route at Faversham. Apart from this missing bridge, much of the old C & W route is identifiable.

Meanwhile the second main section of this total route was under construction at the London end. This consisted of a group of schemes, collectively called the Western or London Extension, aiming at eventual unification into one London to Dover sweep, opening the Continent to Kent, and Kent to the Continent.

First, under a Bill of 1856, came the long Chatham (Strood) to St Mary Cray section, part of a tortuous plan ultimately to reach London. Initially this Bill failed, but it was granted in 1858. As one lineside town's monthly newspaper explained: 'EAST KENT RAILWAY: The contest for an independent route to Dover has just been decided by a Committee of the House of Commons in favour of the East Kent Company by an extension of their line from Strood to St. Mary Cray. The effect is to place in the hands of this company, whose total capital is only two millions, the shortest route by Dover to the Continent. . . . It is stated to save 20 miles to Canterbury . . . and eight or nine to Dover, affording also by means of another line before Parliament, a West End terminus at Pimlico. . . . The time for the purchase of land was limited to two years, and for the completion of the Western Extension and Dover Extension to the 29th of September 1860.'

Beckenham and Bromley were reached, still farther west, by a spur off Norwood on the little West End & Crystal Palace Railway, joining up with the equally diminutive Mid Kent Railway. These works emerged as a series of joints and joins by

19

Invicta, Kent's first railway locomotive, remembered on a Canterbury inn sign.

little companies with big names, to whom the bigger Chatham would ironically have to pay dues if it were ever to enter London.

The temporary terminus of these works, a so-called Bromley station, was the stop now named Shortlands, on the road *to* Bromley, twenty minutes' hard uphill slog to the north. Tracks were initially only single.

On opening day, 3 May 1858, crowds gathered on Martin's Hill to witness the first departure, some say to a salute of guns. The event was duly reported: 'The opening of the Crystal Palace and West End Railway [*sic*] to Bromley took place on Monday May 3rd. The first railway train for passengers and goods left the Shortlands Station at 8.40 am. Those who expected the line to be opened with sound of trumpets and such like ceremony were disappointed; no intimation of its opening was given till the day previous. A goodly number of the inhabitants were on Martin's Hill to witness the starting of the first train, which consisted of four carriages and but few passengers. The station, though progressing rapidly, is far from complete; but, when finished, we hope to see a building which shall be an ornament to the neighbourhood as well as useful to the travelling public.'

By June 1858 timetables had settled down to ten trains each way from Beckenham to London, from 8.10 in the morning to 10.10 at night. Fares ranged on the Mid Kent from one shilling (5p) First Class, through 9d (4p) Second, to only 6d (2½p) Third. From Bromley (Shortlands) to Pimlico, the West End (or West London) & Crystal Palace Railway advertised eight 'up' and seven 'down' trains at fares ranging from 1s 8d (9p) First Class single, down to 1s 3d (6p) Third Class return.

Comparatively commendable speeds were promised: 'These trains usually arrive at the Crystal Palace in twelve minutes, and at Pimlico about 25 minutes later.' There was still chopping and changing from one company's trains to another's, as the time-table admitted (in the small print traditionally reserved for unpalatable truths), in short: 'All the Crystal Palace Trains stop at the Beckenham Junction Station; but Passengers going to London Bridge must wait for Mid Kent Trains at Beckenham if they go from Bromley by any train other than the 8.40 and 9.25 Trains, unless they change trains at Crystal Palace.'

Horse buses were laid on from outlying villages, such as Fownes' Omnibus from Keston, Bromley Common and Bromley town, picking up at the Rising Sun at 9.05, 11.30, 4.05 and 7.50 pm. Additional buses ran between Bromley and Beckenham.

Only two months later, on 5 July 1858, the little Mid Kent Railway pushed its single track forward to the real station for Bromley (now Bromley South), on the site of an old Charity School. It took two more years to reach out one more stop to Bickley.

Fears arose as early as August 1858 as the district became

networked by single tracks. As one local paper pointed out: 'An announcement appeared to the effect that they would run . . . 40 trains per day during the month, and not a little alarm was occasioned at this announcement as they would have to work upon a single line of rails between Shortlands and Beckenham while to make the matter still more alarming at that time no means of telegraphic communication had been provided, so that if the utmost care was not exercised, numerous accidents must be the result.'

Company reports

By September 1858 the EKR was ready to make its report. This was duly repeated in local newspapers along the line, some of which gave substantial extracts describing how the Crays Company had conceded to the East Kent Railway the right to construct the two miles of line between Bickley and St Mary Cray (referred to as 'St Mary's Cray'). The EKR also undertook to double, within twelve months, the adjoining section of track linking Bickley with Bromley, originally opened as a single track. As the report stated: 'The Directors have entered into agreements with the Crays and the West End and Crystal Palace Companies, as to the tolls to be paid for running over their lines, by the East Kent, are to fix the fares, and those companies to receive a mileage proportion of the same, less 20 per cent for locomotive expenses, and wear and tear of rolling stock.'

Plaque at Canterbury (West) commemorating the issue of the world's first railway season tickets in 1834.

NEAR HERE WAS THE TERMINUS OF THE CANTERBURY AND WHITSTABLE RAILWAY, 1830 (GEORGE STEPHENSON, ENGINEER) THE WORLD'S FIRST RAILWAY SEASON TICKETS ISSUED HERE 1834

Approaching the new Kingsferry Bridge to the Isle of Sheppey. Its predecessor carried boat trains to Queenborough and Sheerness Docks.

Local topography. This mainline station recalls the long-gone Kent House which, before the modern boundary changes, was the first house in Kent to be seen by people travelling from London or Surrey.

The Mid Kent also issued an 1858 report, showing 'that the gross receipts earned upon the line during the past half-year amount to £2831. 17s. 8d., shewing an increase of £766. 13s. 6d. upon the corresponding period last year. Notwithstanding the general falling off in receipts on the railways . . . during the last six months, the traffic on this line has steadily improved, and since the opening of the St Mary Cray Railway to Bromley and Southborough Road, on the 1st July, it has shewn such a marked increase that a considerably higher rate of dividend may be anticipated for the next half-year.' The directors could legitimately congratulate themselves on the passing of an Act in the current session of Parliament, for their East Kent Extension from Strood back to St Mary Cray in the Londonward direction, which was expected to bring considerable extra traffic – and profit – to the line.

Yet the novelty of railways wore off amazingly quickly. With the line only two months old, a correspondent was ready to thunder in his local newspaper on the subject of exorbitant parcels charges by rail to Bromley. Trade, in his opinion, should retaliate forthwith by withdrawing its custom in favour of the old-fashioned road carriers who still existed, conveying parcels to London at a considerable reduction in cost.

A major gap was closed in July 1858 when the Mid Kent's Bickley – St Mary Cray length opened, though the company's name was something of a misnomer; if the Medway is Kent's midway point, the Crays are very much at the western edge.

Finally, the LCDR linked up from Rochester Bridge (Strood) past St Mary Cray to Bickley, making possible one uninterrupted journey without changing; on 3 December 1860 trains at last reached Victoria, albeit over other companies' metals for the last fifteen miles or so. In fact, as well as in name, the whole system could then truthfully call itself the London, Chatham & Dover Railway.

It was presumably doubling of track that the Cray newspaper meant when writing in late May 1858 of 'the Mid Kent (St Mary Cray) line which is now being constructed', for tracks were soon doubled almost throughout.

Southborough renamed

The spirit of a terminus like Dover after the arrival of a ferry from the Continent. The accent is on baggage and elegant attire, rather than the rough and tumble of an ordinary busy railway station.

The station between Bromley and St Mary Cray was initially named Southborough or Southborough Road (after a tiny hamlet long since swallowed by suburbia); but by August 1859 agitation for its renaming was already growing. Bickley's local press led the argument: 'Great inconvenience is constantly experienced by there being two Southboroughs on the South Eastern system of

23

Fawkham before the demise of steam. The station lay on the East Kent Railway's Western Extension.

Railway: one near Bromley and the other near Tunbridge [Tonbridge]. Parcels are frequently sent to the wrong station, and persons unacquainted with the locality often take their seats and arrive at a spot far away from their intended destination. . . . To prevent these causes of disappointment and confusion, we suggest a speedy alteration of the name of the station near Bromley. Why not name it "Widmore Station" or "Bickley Station"?' It was the name Bickley that was adopted.

In October 1858 the MKR issued another report, from which we have room only for a few extracts. The main boast was that 'the Directors have the pleasure of stating that, during the six weeks that the Railway has been opened, the gross receipts at the Bromley and Southborough Road stations have amounted to £571. 8s. 9d., which show an average of £95. 5s. per week for passenger traffic alone.' Facilities for passengers, coal and general freight alike were in the process of being improved at Bromley at the behest of the South Eastern Company. During this financial year Parliament had also sanctioned a Bill promoted by the East Kent for their promised extension from Strood westwards to join up with the Bromley & St Mary Cray Railway, bringing one single route from the Medway to London a step nearer.

However, not everybody was enchanted by trains. On the same page as the new railway timetables there were often advertise-

Herne Hill station, first major junction out of Victoria, in a mêlée of horses, carts and cabs during its SECR days.

ments for coach and carriage builders – a reminder that for every town connected to the railway there were ten small villages which were not.

The LCDR now had the convenience of a through route, spoiled only by the need to run its final miles over other people's property (even the tiny Victoria Station & Pimlico Company took its cut, as owner of the terminus bridges and approaches), but any means of reaching London was better than none.

The Chatham (as the total route was colloquially called) was now open to the three types of traffic that characterize it today: coal and freight, commuters, and cross-Channel passengers.

The little Mid Kent's next report was full of bright hopes and self-congratulations, including such statements as: 'The traffic of the line is now in course of development, and the proprietors may feel assured that each succeeding half-year will continue to show a steady increase in receipts. The total net income for the half-year available for dividend is £1,713. 2s. 4d., and out of this the Directors recommend a dividend at the rate of £4 per cent per annum, leaving £85. 18s. 9d. to be carried to the credit of the next account.'

Populations rocketed around the rails; Bromley's, for example, expanded from 5505 at the 1861 Census to 33,646 over the next fifty years.

An impatient American tourist sees England for the first time. (Reproduction by courtesy of *Punch*.)

When this picture was taken, Shepherds Well near Dover was set in deep country. Today it serves as a rural suburb of the port.

Tourism begins

Money was short, but it bought a lot even when a family man's income was scarcely £3 a week. A Dover day trip cost just half-a-crown (2s 6d, or 12½p), and Canterbury could be reached in about two hours. From Beckenham to London cost only 6d (2½p) return, Third Class. The world was suddenly Everyman's oyster, and he made the most of it.

However, Everyman was not entirely happy with actual travelling conditions, any more than he is today. Within a year of the railway's opening one newspaper reported in disgruntlement: 'We believe a memorial has been presented to the Directors [of the Mid Kent] signed by the annual ticket holders and other passengers, with reference to the Second Class Carriages attached to the early morning and other Trains on this Line. The Carriages in some cases are worse than Third Class, and have been a source of complaint for some time past.'

Country landowners had to be compensated for land commandeered for tracks. W.W. Mosyer of St Mary Cray, and George Reeves, a builder of that village, were awarded £200 and £10 respectively by the East Kent Western Extension, within ten months of its opening.

A proposed extension to pretty Farnborough, south of Bromley, was abandoned as early as January 1859, according to another report which said: 'West End of London and Crystal Palace Railway: The promoters . . . have given notice of their

THE HYPNOTIC STEWARD.

(Specially engaged for the Cross-Channel Service.)

["Dr. Paul Farez asserts that he has found in hypnotism an absolutely infallible remedy for sea-sickness and similar discomforts."—*Daily Paper.*]

As the *Punch* artist saw travellers off the Continental boat-train settling down for the crossing, with Dover Castle in the background, in 1898. (Reproduction by courtesy of *Punch*.)

intention to apply to Parliament next Session for an Act by which favour will be sought to abandon a portion of the railway and works authorised by the West End of London and Crystal Palace Railway (Extension to Farnborough) Act 1854'.

Regular travellers quickly got to know their local station staff, congratulating them on landmarks in their lives and contributing to presentations when they left or retired. A presentation was news in the 1850s, worthy of reporting in such phrases as these: 'We have to record another gratifying instance of desert in a Railway Official and recognition of it by the Public, in the presentation to Mr. Allen, who has been a Guard on the Mid Kent Line from its opening, of a small purse of silver, contributed chiefly by regular travellers. . . We understand a similar subscription has been entered into by the Catford Bridge passengers, the above Officer being universally respected in his line of life.'

Locomotives were small in those early days, and initially not

27

But for the stock, Victoria has the look of a modern terminus in this picture. No. 449 backs out after departure of the train it originally headed in. The train on the extreme right may well be a boat train, since its carriages have roof headboards.

even the EKR's own; they borrowed some small Hawthorn engines from the Great Northern Railway. Six new 4-4-0 saddle tanks were ordered for 1858, but these were also small and not particularly powerful.

It remained for the next decade to create a real railway from these somewhat haphazard beginnings.

2
Early Days in Kent

The 1860s and 1870s were decades of consolidation, of settling into routine, and of learning lessons from lesser problems and greater disasters.

For the first time the South Eastern Railway found the London Chatham & Dover a rival instead of a poor relation, as the latter possessed its own London terminus, a prospering outer London network, and a shorter route to Dover. The SER scarcely helped itself when, in 1862, it let slip a chance of carrying Continental mail to government contract, leaving this option to the LCDR; foreign mail offered prestige if not profit.

After losing its mail contract, the SER moved most European business to Folkestone, thus leaving its rival more or less in possession of Dover, the busier of these two ports. However, the SER continued into Dover by its own route for everyday traffic.

Continental traffic steadily expanded. Principal boat trains had the Chatham's best coaching stock, ever striving to outdo the SER, like Kent schoolboys 'doing each others' dags'. The SER alone mustered eight Continentals a day, with onward cross-Channel links. The LCDR also ran a few specials to its lesser Kent port of Queenborough, on the Sheerness line into Sheppey.

Locomotive stock remained haphazard through much of this early period. Borrowings from other systems included a contractor's 0-4-0T loaned for Sheerness; secondhand engines came in, including a freight engine renamed *Swale*, after the narrow waterway which makes Sheppey an island.

Cash crisis, and fears for a tunnel

Money was always short, forcing the acquisition of secondhand bargains. From Hawthorn came a couple of 0-6-0 engines, followed by four Stephenson 4-4-0s, initially intended for the Middle East. These in turn were disembowelled and reassembled as side-tanks for further duty.

At the London end of the route, unfounded fears mounted for the major engineering work of Penge tunnel, nearly a mile long, burrowing deeply underneath the hill on which stood the Crystal Palace. Even today, this is an awesome plunge underground; but at that time, with smoke and smuts swirling over hastily closed windows, it seemed a veritable dungeon. Nearly 210,000 cubic

VICTORIA STATION (S. E. & CHATHAM Rly.) LONDON.

FROM THIS BUSY TERMINUS BOOKINGS ARE MADE TO MANY OF THE POPULAR SEASIDE RESORTS ON THE SOUTH COAST AND TO THE CONTINENT via DOVER AND FOLKESTONE

ADJOINING IS THE GROSVENOR HOTEL AND THE WEST END TERMINUS OF THE LONDON BRIGHTON AND SOUTH COAST RAILWAY.

SHORTEST ROUTE TO PARIS AND THE CONTINENT and SEA PASSAGE ONE HOUR. Advertisement boards at Victoria emphasize that this is the departure point for Kentish boat trains and Dover connections. There is still some allegiance to an old bargain with the GWR.

yards of heavy clay were gouged out for this bore; much of this was made into bricks for its lining and thus carried back into the tunnel. Penge tunnel would soon collapse, proclaimed the pessimists, and bury a whole train underground. Queen Victoria allegedly disliked Penge tunnel, or even feared it, and that (according to local legend) was why the alternative Catford Loop was built along the flatter Ravensbourne Valley.

Penge tunnel occurred on the LCDR's newer Metropolitan Extension of 1860, which opened up the present direct line as far as Herne Hill. In August 1862 the continuation thence to Victoria opened, while a connection off Blackfriars to Herne Hill was also made. The Blackfriars addition helped open up Fleet Street to railways, carrying newspapers and newsmen at all hours, until eventually trains ran all night over the Catford Loop right through to the 1960s. This line reached its London destination on 21 December 1864 at a terminus whose abandoned outline is still visible near the present Blackfriars.

The line was then opened across the River Thames to Ludgate Hill (later St Paul's). The station, similar in design to the original Blackfriars (on the Surrey instead of the north bank) was opened to traffic before full completion, with only two platforms working. The opening of this station completed the so-called Metropolitan Extension.

During the same month the rival SER found itself less happily

30

The Station, St. Mary Cray

Few places have changed more than St Mary Cray, one of the first stations opened on the Western Extension in the 1850s. What was the country-side around it is today a vast modern industrial town, and the station of four platforms has been heavily modernized.

placed, defending the case of 'Craker *v.* South Eastern Railway'. To quote one of many reports: 'This was an action brought against the SER Company for false imprisonment. . . . The action arose out of the loss of a purse at the Folkestone Junction station, where the plaintiff was porter in the month of August 1863; and its having been suggested that the plaintiff (who had given up the purse at the time to a gentleman by whom it was claimed) had appropriated it to his own use, although the General Manager of the company had written to the owner of the purse, stating that he had no reason to doubt the plaintiff's honesty, a detective officer named Strickland was sent down to Folkestone to make enquiries and subsequently, upon his report, to apprehend the plaintiff. The plaintiff, after having been taken from home, and been locked up all night without any food, was taken before the Borough Magistrates at Folkestone.' The wronged porter won his case, with damages of £85, a substantial sum for the period.

Continental traffic expands

Despite longer journey mileage, the rival SER still retained some position in coastal and Continental traffic, but a new sea route planned for 1867, cutting time off the port-to-Paris leg, enabled the LCDR to catch up; thereafter the LCDR was the recognized gateway to Paris and further south, through Dover.

31

Canterbury seen from a train in 1980; a familiar view to every traveller in and out of Dover.

In July 1862 a full service had begun via Calais, using the mail boats also as ferries. There was no Dover – Boulogne crossing, as the French railways sided with the SER and its Folkestone – Boulogne service; finally, by 1865, the two British interests had forged a more sensible understanding on Continental working, as the unnecessary rivalry had depleted both their coffers. By the same year the LCDR's bread-and-butter services, as opposed to European 'jam', had also marginally increased throughout what is now called the commuter belt. Even on Sundays, St Mary Cray boasted seven 'up' and seven 'down' services, with the rider that 'all the Up Trains from St Mary Cray call at Bickley about seven minutes later'; a four- or five-minute run today. The Sevenoaks branch out of Swanley offered eight trains each way on weekdays and six on Sundays, while the Mid Kent section of the main line, taking Bickley as a terminus instead of a passing stop, gave a service that is not available today – from Bickley and Bromley to Beckenham and thence by a spur onto the New Beckenham – Lewisham – Charing Cross line (a connection for which workers today plead in vain). However, Sunday services were very poor; from Bickley only at 9.07 am, or at 7.24, 9.13 and 9.54 pm (the latter presumably serving Fleet Street's overnight editions rather than Everyman). Fownes's Keston Omnibus continued to provide a connection to Bromley from the country.

32

Reporting the profits

Missing the train! A J.B. Clark cartoon in *Home Words*. The presence of heavy luggage suggests a boat-train line rather than suburbia.

Local papers habitually reprinted company reports in detail. We thus have an LCDR half-yearly report for mid-1865 from which to select a few extracts: 'The traffic certainly was not as large as they had reason to expect which was owing to two causes. In the first place, the works at Victoria Station were not complete, which occasioned much inconvenience to the public and much loss to the company. The next and most important cause was the want of the completion of the link line with the Metropolitan Extension line. . . The London Chatham and Dover was ready to join the Underground Railway now, and their line had been surveyed and approved by the Government Inspector. Their expenses had been very great, but the company were obliged to give the public the same accommodation that their rivals afforded. Their traffic had increased during the past half-year to the extent of £10,000 . . . The traffic on the Crystal Palace line had so augmented that during the past week it was four times as much as it was during the first week of its opening. They had come to an understanding with the South Eastern Company by which they had put an end to all damaging competition and their energies would be directed to the improvement of the line and stock . . . The June half-year showed a net surplus increase of £10,182.'

In the same issue the South Eastern made its own declaration, limited mainly to finance, partly in connection with Continental

Another cartoon from *Home Words*; a not greatly exaggerated view of freight handling at the turn of the century. A French label suggests that this could have been the Port of Dover.

33

traffic: 'Gross receipts £630,434.16s. 6d., the receipts from the steamboat traffic, amounting to £27,474.12s. are included. . . . Last year the gross receipts for the corresponding period was £596,894.10s. 4d. There is thus an increase of £33,540.6s. 2d. on the income for the past six months. The principal items in this increase have been as follows: 438,924 more passengers were conveyed, augmenting the receipts from this source by £19,294; £6,324 extra accrued from the merchandise traffic; and £6,781 under the head of rents and sundries which have principally arisen from the letting of arches and property along the new portion of the line.' Against receipts were set expenses including 'working of the steam packet service £13,991.2s. 10d.'

Accidental death on the line gained a certain panache in the reporting, as the public developed a disconcerting habit of wandering onto railways and being killed in a lurid manner. We have room to select only one (from November 1865) as illustration, when near Bickley station a local carpenter unthinkingly walked onto the track as the 5.50 train from London was passing. 'His head being literally smashed, death must have been instantaneous' commented his local paper. He was taken to Bromley police station but later removed to the Bell Inn pending an inquest. He was a curiously elusive character, having no means of identification but a silver ring on one finger and a pencil in his pocket.

Small wonder, then, that regular collisions between people and steam engines even entered local lineside lore in such bloodthirsty lines as 'Johnny On The Railway', rudely chanted out:

> Johnny on the railway, picking up stones,
> Along comes an engine and bites off his nose;
> 'Oh' says Johnny, 'That's not fair.'
> 'Oh' says the engine, 'I don't care.'

The Beckenham disaster

Semaphore signals have now given way almost everywhere to colour-light signalling.

In January 1866 the LCDR's fairly humdrum suburban fetching and carrying was rudely interrupted by the line's most serious accident, spectacular enough to be copiously reported in *The Times* for the whole nation to murmur over. To extract the salient points from a lengthy report published the next day, 15 January 1866: 'One of the bridges spanning a running stream in the vicinity of Beckenham gave way yesterday morning at an early hour, and precipitated a goods train into an obscure stream, where the engine and tender, with 13 trucks, lie buried in one conglomerate mass at the moment of writing. The midnight train from Victoria and Blackfriars to Chatham, and the early goods train following, had passed over the bridge in question safely, but the later goods train, due at Beckenham Junction shortly before 4 o'clock yesterday morning, was that to which the accident occurred. After passing the Penge station, the London Chatham

34

Ancient and modern at Queenborough on the Sheerness Branch, opened off the main line in 1860. Behind the brambles on the right the one-time Leysdown Branch is closed and overgrown. Sheerness trains still join the main line at Sittingbourne.

and Dover Railway traverses a district which is here and there interspersed by brooks tributary to the Ravensbourne River. These brooks are for the most part crossed by flat iron girder bridges, and one of these, within a couple of hundred yards of the Beckenham Junction, was the unfortunate scene of the disaster. The train to which the accident occurred left Blackfriars station at half past 1 o'clock yesterday morning, and after the usual stoppages at Herne Hill and other stations to pick up trucks, was approaching the Beckenham Junction at five minutes to 4 o'clock when, without any previous warning of danger, the engine and tender, with 13 of the foremost trucks, were precipitated into a stream known as the Rusher Brook, ordinarily a mere ditch but swollen by the late flood into a small river. The engine fell on its right side, and by a most fortunate accident the driver was thrown into an adjoining meadow, where he sustained only temporary injuries. The stoker, who most probably was attending to his break, was less fortunate, and, falling with the engine, was buried under it, and his body had not been extricated at 6 o'clock last evening. The guard, who was travelling in a tender immediately behind the engine, suffered severe contusions but a projecting girder saved his life.' Curiously, only one part of the bridge actually collapsed, the cause being the aftermath of heavy snow and floods. The other remaining line could be made safe with the aid of gangs of hard-working navvies. All day they laboured, while passengers

35

A sign dating from the years between the LCDR/SER amalgamation of 1899 and the major railway grouping that took place in 1923. Such relics are fast disappearing.

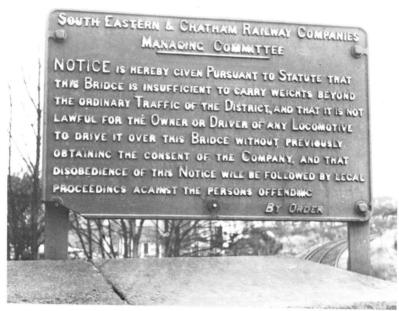

SOUTH EASTERN & CHATHAM RAILWAY COMPANIES MANAGING COMMITTEE

NOTICE IS HEREBY GIVEN PURSUANT TO STATUTE THAT THIS BRIDGE IS INSUFFICIENT TO CARRY WEIGHTS BEYOND THE ORDINARY TRAFFIC OF THE DISTRICT, AND THAT IT IS NOT LAWFUL FOR THE OWNER OR DRIVER OF ANY LOCOMOTIVE TO DRIVE IT OVER THIS BRIDGE WITHOUT PREVIOUSLY OBTAINING THE CONSENT OF THE COMPANY. AND THAT DISOBEDIENCE OF THIS NOTICE WILL BE FOLLOWED BY LEGAL PROCEEDINGS AGAINST THE PERSONS OFFENDING

BY ORDER

were conveyed in two halves of their journeys, getting out at the bridge, walking over the undamaged section, and joining another train waiting on the opposite side.

Next day the bridge was still being shored up, as the foundations of the central arch had been completely washed away. By two o'clock an empty test train could be safely eased across, but the actual wreckage lay as tangled as ever. Large heaps of smashed wood and twisted rubble had still to be removed before the body of the dead stoker could be recovered; it was wedged between the guard's van and the remains of the collapsed central pier, lying almost in the water.

For the LCDR, 1866 thus opened badly. More ill fortune lay ahead, when its monetary affairs took a turn for the worse, aggravated by a peculiar early arrangement with its contractors as shareholders. Disaster was staved off, but the end of the LCDR's independent life was not far ahead. With the turn of the century both the SER and the LCDR would lose their old identities, and move forward together instead of in opposition.

3
The 'Land 'em Smash 'em and Over'

Towards the end of the nineteenth century the LCDR appears to have first acquired one of those usually derogatory nicknames which travellers bestowed on their local railways, such as the 'Slow Dirty Jerky Railway' (SDJR or Somerset & Dorset Joint Railway), the 'Blaze and Stoke' (Basingstoke) or, nearer home, the 'Slow and Easy Railway' (SER). To the London Chatham & Dover went the unflattering epithet 'Land 'em Smash 'em and Over' – not inappropriate considering its employees' unconcern in throwing crates marked 'Fragile, With Care' into vans with resounding crashes.

Workmen's tickets and conditions

Workmen's tickets were a late nineteenth-century attribution to the LCDR, by favour of Parliament. With these tickets, workers were carried in overcrowded discomfort at ungodly hours to London, the catch being that their journeys must finish before the main rush hour even began, usually by 8 am. However, the fares were so low as to justify this battle against the alarm clock. That special workmen's services existed before 1870 becomes clear from a reader's letter to one of the commuter area's popular journals: 'Sir: I believe it is an undisputed fact that the London Chatham and Dover Railway Company are short of money; also that there are many houses standing empty in Bromley for want of tenants, and that there are numbers of working men in London wanting houses, but cannot have them because of the expense of coming to and fro. Now, Mr Editor, what is there to prevent the LC&DR Co. putting money in their pockets by continuing the workmen's train from Penge on to Beckenham and Bromley, thereby benefiting themselves and others at the same time without any (or, at least, very little) extra expense, as the workman's train starts from Bickley and stops at Bromley and Beckenham?'

Rivalry continued, or even increased, between the two principal Kent companies, not helped by new friction between their respective General Managers and Chairmen, J.S. Forbes of the LCDR and Edward Watkin, the 'railway king' of the SER. Their previously vaunted agreement on Continental working at one end of the line proved but a flash in the pan at the other, particularly after Watkin proposed (and actually started) a Channel Tunnel. In

This footbridge was added to Beckenham Junction following complaints from the public, and a death in the 1870s.

the mid-1870s the SER plunged into a new boat-train venture, opening up dreary Port Victoria on the Isle of Grain opposite Sheerness, claimed to be the nearest deep-water port to London and for a time adopted by Queen Victoria and the Kaiser for berthing their royal yachts and boarding their royal trains. Flushing, in Holland, was the SER's destination; a service lately resurrected by Olau Line from adjacent Sheerness.

The best rolling stock was reserved for boat trains by both companies, including the Chatham's extravagant Palace Car, including not only a smoking-room and saloon, but even a bridal compartment.

Enigma and Variations

Not until 1869 did Longhedge works produce a new as opposed to reconditioned locomotive, the *Enigma* (2-4-0) allegedly so named because of certain parties' doubts about the Chatham's ability to pay for it. The name *Enigma* was eventually bestowed on the rest of its class.

Railways had no monopoly of transport, however. Into the 1870s, outlying districts sent produce to market by four-footed horse-power, and steam came onto the highway as well as to the railway. We know of what was virtually a goods train without rails

A suburban electric train about to plunge into Penge Tunnel. Dire prognostications of collapse heralded the tunnel's opening, and it was allegedly so detested by Queen Victoria that the alternative Catford Loop was built to avoid the steep Sydenham Hill.

Penge East in the early morning. The suburban third rail electrification can be clearly seen in this photograph.

No. 17 coasts into a now unrecognizable country station in about 1915.

serving the Cray district despite the existence of St Mary Cray station, as *The Cray*, a short-lived local paper, reported in July 1872: 'THE STEAM TRACTION COMPANY: Our readers resident on the old London and Maidstone turnpike road . . . will have seen and heard a locomotive travelling on this road slowly, with large heavy waggons behind. This is the new train started by the Company. Every alternate night the engine, of 12 horse power, travels to London, taking farm produce, returning to the country the following night, drawing London manure. We are told this one engine draws down to the Crays and Farnborough, in one journey, upwards of twenty tons weight of manure, and can take up to London the same tonnage of agricultural produce. . . Fancy a train, as we see them on the railway, taking to the common roads, and you will have some idea of the train started by the Kent Traction Company.'

Timetables of the 1870s showed dramatic increases in weekday services, although Sunday services remained poor with only one morning and one evening train from Dover to St Mary Cray and Bickley. By then the present continuation to Herne Hill and Victoria was operational. On the final stretch of the extension from Herne Hill three extra stations existed (long since lost), Camberwell New Road, Walworth Road and Borough Road, spaced close together. Blackfriars Bridge station stood at that bridge's southern end; its site is still identifiable and its entrance drive is intact, together with the painted inscriptions 'Dover Shed No. 1' and

'By your leave, sir'; a cartoon from *Railway Servants* showing the perils of rail travel in 1883.

'Mileage Shed No. 4', and massive ironwork including rusted crests of the three namesake towns and cities. From Bickley, still the main starting point, weekday services ran from five in the morning to 10.30 at night. Faversham and Sittingbourne offered reasonable Victoria services. Altogether twenty-four trains off this route alone reached Victoria daily; few by modern standards, but at that time a great improvement.

But still John Citizen did not learn that trains were dangerous, even though the local papers were full of sudden deaths under steam engines. John Citizen also complained continuously against the railway; there were in particular grouses about the inconvenience of Beckenham station, where people were hurried from the London end of the platforms right back to the 'down' end, up flights of steps, and all the way down again, only to traverse the whole length of a platform once more. Passengers for London Bridge and other stations on the South Eastern complained of an actual risk to human life in the sheer stress and physical effort forced on older and weaker men among them by the daily stampede. At Beckenham passengers out of Bromley were compelled to change from the LCDR to the South Eastern line, more often than not arriving just as their connection was pulling away. At least one collapse and death during this daily scrimmage reached the local coroner's court, and the travelling public did not willingly accept the verdict of 'death from natural causes'. At the very least, they believed, his death had been accelerated by over-

Shortlands Junction photographed from the only possible viewpoint: the window of a Victoria-bound train. The Catford Loop is to the right.

41

The London Chatham & Dover terminus at Victoria, probably just after the First World War. The layout is similar today.

exertion at Beckenham. Eventually a better footbridge was added to reduce this trial upon the travelling public.

Railways and suburban growth

With improving timetables, such villages as St Mary Cray and Bickley began to grow, though they were still only hamlets compared with their sizes today. Bickley was described in 1875 as 'a hamlet and ecclesiastical district, pop. 623 . . . on the LC & D or Mid Kent branch of the South Eastern Railway . . . a good deal changed by building operations, the inevitable result of railway facilities'. Swanley had 'grown into local importance since it has become the junction station of the Sevenoaks and main lines of the LC & D Railway'.

Public services meanwhile continued to range between the erratic and the luxurious. We find special trains being laid on for such events as the funerals of those whose families could afford big money, such as the owners of the big St Mary Cray paper mills, duly recounted in a local paper in August 1875. While bathing in Paris, William Joynson, grandson of the mill owner and a joint heir to this prosperous business, was accidentally drowned during a Grand Tour of Europe in company with his local vicar. His body was returned to England and St Mary Cray, but the actual funeral took place at High Wycombe in Buckinghamshire, whence he was

42

conveyed by special train at considerable expense.

Animosity and agreement alternated in the affairs of the SER and LCDR. 'We are told that a provisional agreement has been settled by the Joint Committee of the South Eastern and the London Chatham and Dover Railway Companies for a fusion of the net profits of the two undertakings and for an interchange of traffic and friendly working at all points; we do not pretend to understand the exact meaning of the statement, and it would probably be an error to suppose that it was intended anyone should at once understand it perfectly . . . it requires a double or triple sanction before it can become complete and binding' stated the *Bromley Record* with an air of suspicion. 'The war of competition will cease, but otherwise there is to be no change. This may be a misapprehension of the brief announcement which has been authoritatively put forward, and we can only hazard it subject to all possible corrections on the part of the Joint Committee', the report concluded.

Chairman Forbes considered his company had done handsomely for 1874, having made a 'very large increase in the receipts'. Plans for lines and sidings off the main line into Chatham Dockyard were well advanced, according to the company's report: 'The necessary agreement had been made with regard to Chatham Dockyard, and the company had been guaranteed against losses. The line would be opened in the course of this or the next year, and the large quantity of goods conveyed

In the early years of the East Kent Railway a branch and networks of sidings were thrown out to serve Chatham dockyard, seen here on a public Navy Day in about 1957. Men in uniform always crowded the platforms at Victoria before the departure of a Chatham train.

THE STATION, SELLING.

Selling, a remote village among the hop-gardens, some miles from Canterbury. Hoppers' bushel-baskets stand stacked against the waiting-room wall.

into Chatham would give them large indirect advantages.' This branch finally opened in February 1877.

Holborn Viaduct and Snow Hill opened

Holborn Viaduct station and the now closed Low Level station (Snow Hill) were completed by 1874. Entrances to the semi-underground Snow Hill were to be from both sides of the new viaduct and from Snow Hill itself, the subterranean platforms being linked by staircases from the booking offices above ground. New goods warehouses opened at Holborn, storing Kentish hops in quantity among other cargoes, easing some previously difficult storage problems. Hops also brought a good annual revenue from the transport of pickers in their thousands out to the Kent hop-gardens; they were conveyed in spartan specials made up of the worst rolling stock, jammed in with their goods, chattels, babies, clothes, pots and pans, and squeeze-box accordions for accompanying loud sing-songs on the journey.

Freight services reflected the general low level of costs compared with today – a hundredweight of goods could be conveyed for just 6s 8d (approximately 33p), and a ton of hay could be weighed for transit for just 2d (scarcely 1p).

44

Victoria at a time when it was two separate terminus stations: for LCDR (later SECR) and LB & SCR. Note the horse-drawn cabs on the left of the photograph.

The SECR part of Victoria terminus, with a horse-drawn bus about to leave. Ports and boat-train station names run across the front: Calais, Ostend, Folkestone, Boulogne, Queenborough and Flushing. EXPRESS ROUTES TO THE CONTINENT gives emphasis to Continental rather than local services.

The biggest engineering work on the Sevenoaks branch, which leaves the Dover line at Swanley, where it is taken over the high viaduct near Eynsford. This photograph was taken in about 1952, but the scene is virtually unchanged today.

First hints of amalgamation

Premature speculation on possible amalgamation instead of competition between the LCDR and the SER began in 1875, when the Kent press put forward its arguments: 'The *Railway News* says that the statement that the arrangements for the fusion of the South Eastern and the London Chatham and Dover Companies had been completed, and that the particulars would be immediately announced, is, to say the least, premature. The basis of the arrangements was understood to have been that of division of net profits in the proportion of the gross receipts of the respective companies last year. We believe that some difficulty has arisen as to the interpretation to be put upon the proposed agreement, which it is not improbable may prevent any further progress in this direction. . . The point in dispute involves a considerable sum and it is stated that one of the parties will not consent to any modification of the proposal, and that the other will not accept it in its present form.'

If suburban services were only just adequate, prestige main-line workings showed off the two companies' best engines and rolling stock, still forever 'keeping up with the Joneses'. Directly the SER began in 1877 its new Granville Special Private Express to Faversham and then away from the Dover line to Ramsgate, the LCDR responded with a confusingly similar Granville Express, Granville being a much used Ramsgate local place-name.

Similar striving produced for the Chatham in 1889 a special afternoon boat train for the Paris Exhibition, the *Paris Mail Limited*; whereupon the SER retaliated with a Club Train. Passengers enjoyed these luxuries only in small numbers, and neither train lasted long.

Passengers apart, one of Kent's staple freight commodities was

A CASE OF NEGLECT.

A cartoon from *Railway Servants*, published in the 1880s, showing a station scene with a poor old lady being neglected while a rich young woman is fawned upon by station staff.

46

coal from the big Kent coalfield at Snowdown and Betteshanger (colloquially Betty Shanger), a far more universal necessity then than it is today, with every train, ship, factory, office and home burning it in large quantities. Not least among the more utility LCDR locomotives' duties was transporting coal for their own and their stablemates' fireboxes and tenders.

The 1880s coasted towards the nineties. For Everyman they were times of immensely hard work for poor pay, and of a fierce search for cheap pleasure and entertainment, from the music halls to the seaside. For the LCDR and the SER the nineties would bring a complete reversal of fortune; through the liberation afforded by trains to enjoy himself, Everyman had discovered a new identity; on the other hand, the South Eastern and the Chatham were to lose their separate identities, and with them their old squabbles, once and for all.

4
Turn of the Century

The late nineteenth century brought rapid movement towards eventual agreement between the previously warring South Eastern and the Chatham; but first came news, from all quarters of the system, of more everyday matters.

In 1878 a natural event occurred that permanently shaped the track's course at one point; a great flood turned the Ravensbourne Valley into one huge lake of deep dirty water. Hedges, walls and fences were submerged, and the railway was completely covered between Shortlands and Bromley. Early business trains got through, after which the line became so dangerously undermined and waterlogged as to be closed indefinitely. Fortunately, little housing existed there at that time but the line was a serious consideration. Today strangers still ponder why the tracks here run for about a mile along a seemingly unnecessary embankment; the 1878 flood is the answer.

The winter of 1881 was little better, slow to start but vicious when it finally arrived. A very severe frost set in about halfway through January, followed by the worst blizzards for many years. Snow-laden gales lashed ceaselessly for twenty-four hours, spraying the world with a fine powdery snow that almost blinded drivers and pedestrians. Deep drifts halted all railway traffic on the Bromley Direct (SER) line early on the first afternoon, but it was reopened the following day; on the Mid Kent near Catford Bridge three complete trains were snowed in, unable to move, and travellers were forced to walk the rest of the way to Beckenham in appalling conditions. However, trains between Bromley and London on the LCDR managed somehow to force their way through, though extremely late.

Summer day excursions to France, much as we now know them, were practicable by the 1880s, albeit allowing little time ashore. Calais, from Dover, was popular with works outings, of which we have an example in 'Rogers's Excursion' when about four hundred people travelled together for a cheap flying visit to France. The party arrived at Dover at eleven in the morning and crossed to Calais in the *Maid of Kent*. Enough time was then available for them to visit some of the French port's places of interest before returning. They were back in London's suburbia by ten that evening.

In 1882 the Dover approaches were improved by a loop at

RAILWAY STATION, GILLINGHAM, KENT.

Station staff pose for the novelty of a group photograph early in the twentieth century on the platform of the now unrecognizable Gillingham station. Yards and sheds to the left are, unfortunately, just out of picture.

Kearsney, opened on 1 July; but a more ambitious scheme was perforce abandoned. This would have connected the suburbs with Eastbourne via Hayes and Keston, leaving at Shortlands Junction. Cash, as usual, was the obstacle, since this was a difficult terrain to engineer economically.

The Ivy Bridge disaster

1882 also saw the worst disaster on the LCDR as a separate company, the collapse of the Ivy Bridge near Bromley, which killed seven men and orphaned several children. Many columns of reportage were devoted to this calamity, of which the only reasonably concise account appeared in the *Bromley Record* for 1 December 1882: 'On Friday the 24th [November] one of the most fearful catastrophes that ever occurred in Bromley happened on the London Chatham and Dover Railway, through the collapse of a bridge situated about 300 yards to the north [actually east] of Bromley station. . . . On the previous day a grave defect was discovered to exist in the structure, and as it gave ominous signs of a collapse it was decided by Mr. Hewett, the engineer, that the bridge should be pulled down. Gangs of men were got together for this purpose, but at about midnight, as they were taking some of the top off, the pier on the Down side, which had been slipping, suddenly gave way and precipitated several tons of masonry onto the rails. It so happened that several men were at work on the top,

49

Faversham station in about 1905. The children posing in the middle of the road knew that only the occasional horse and cart would be around.

and some fell with the debris, but beyond a slight bruising they were not otherwise injured. Singularly enough the pier on the Up side and an arch connecting it with the bank remained intact, and to all appearance so strong that at six o'clock on Friday morning, when the Up line was cleared, several trains were allowed to pass, and the men having left off for refreshments, eight of them entered a hut under the arch to partake of breakfast. Whilst they were there the remaining portion of the bridge fell without the least warning and completely buried the poor fellows. Assistance was at once procured and the men were taken out in about half an hour, but fearfully battered and injured, and the only one alive was Richard Banks, a young man of St. Mary Cray.'

This bridge was appropriately named, since its festoons of ivy had hidden its parlous condition. Nor was its imminent collapse apparent, for though 'the men were warned not to go under the bridge on the previous night . . . after those two [arches] fell the other arch seemed secure, and no one apparently apprehended danger'. Yet somebody on the line *had* sensed that danger, and sent a telegram to the Engineer's Office at Victoria, from where Hewett the resident engineer immediately set out for the scene; he saw no immediate peril either, and merely 'left two men to watch it and returned to town'. He did, however, have second thoughts; he returned at evening and remained on watch all night. At midnight he saw the first section fall and block the 'down' road, and forthwith ordered its controlled demolition, out of which work the final tragedy developed.

50

Bromley South Station.

Bromley.

A bewhiskered Edwardian bobby stands guard at Bromley South station, while a top-hatted gentleman looks on. Although the railings went for salvage in the Second World War and the front of the building has been modernized, the general look of the place is still recognizable today. There is still an entrance to the former freight yards at the right.

The inquest occupied several sessions, where the ivy's fatal cover was discussed, with the conclusion that 'there was a great deal of ivy over the bridge, and that might have covered some defects'. Even the men's conversation was reconstructed from survivors' accounts, such as that of Jonathan King, labourer, who related that 'a man called "Ginger" told him the bridge had fallen, and he walked up the line and went into the hut about twenty minutes to seven o'clock. Witness said to Harford [a victim]: "it is not safe in here", and he replied "Why not? It is as safe for us as for you". There was a fire in the hut and the men were warming their tea. A train was signalled on, and Hartford said to Tuitt, "Ain't you going to run out this time, Johnny?" Tuitt looked up and said "No, I don't think I shall". None of the men in the hut said they had been warned'. The verdict from eighteen local traders sworn in as a jury, was short and simple: 'Accidental death' with the rider, 'That in the opinion of the jury there was an error in judgement on the part of those responsible that proper means were not taken to secure the south arch by struts or otherwise'.

Even then the tragedy was not ended, for only a few months later a 'Shocking fatality at St. Mary Cray' claimed the son of one of the dead men, leaving his mother broken under this double bereavement. His was a typical death on the line, as a platelayer. As two trains approached from opposite directions and the other men moved aside, the victim stood on the 'up' side of the rails as the Maidstone express was passing and he was struck a savage blow. His mates ran to him immediately, but he was already dead.

51

An ungainly structure covering
the platforms and lines,
probably at Canterbury.

The replacement for Ivy Bridge
at Bromley South, which
disastrously collapsed in 1882.
Even today there is a weight
limit on traffic over the bridge.

'Deceased was only 19 years of age, and had since his father's death been the support of his mother', lamented the Cray press.

Not until early in 1884 were the large proceeds of local collections finally declared and their use outlined in a letter under Mr Maynard's signature, he being the Bromley stationmaster: 'Donations . . . made a total of £494.15s. 10d. . . . and the St. Mary Cray committee £88.8s. 6d. and by Mr. Woodhams, Station Master of St. Mary Cray, £148.14s. 6d., making a gross total of £731.15s. 10d.' From this fund £10 was given to a bereaved father; £50 was invested for Banks, the injured survivor; annuities were bought for 'the five widows and three children of St. Mary Cray and Orpington'; and one child was placed in the Home for Little Boys at Farningham, farther down the Dover line.

'Doing each others' dags'

The SER, doing the LCDR's 'dags' as usual, stated as its latest aim of 1883, 'a fixed service between London and Paris instead of a tidal one'. In this report some alarming decreases in revenue were confessed by Sir Edward Watkin, with over £5000 less taken in passenger fares while expenses rose by over £16,000. Working expenses included £5841 spent on 'locomotive power' and £3567 on steam boats.

Despite these gloomy figures, train services into London increased dramatically at this period. The LCDR did its part, with services from five in the morning until midnight in the outer suburbs of Swanley and St Mary Cray, with nearly fifty 'up' and fifty 'down' services in between on an average weekday.

Efficient (or allegedly efficient) services were the backbone of every suburban estate agent's advertising in the eighties; to quote but a handful of examples: 'Within ten minutes' walk of Beckenham station, whence there is a constant and quick service of trains to all parts of London'; or again: 'Bijou detached house close to the railway station'; or yet again: 'Kent House station is on the London Chatham and Dover Railway, and London can easily be reached in 30 minutes'.

July 1892 brought the opening of the long Nunhead to Shortlands section of the Catford Loop, then and now the main alternative route through suburbia towards Dover; with no tunnels and no loading restrictions, the Loop allowed a fast run through to the junction at Shortlands and thence back onto the main line, much used by coastal expresses and Dover boat trains.

The 1899 amalgamation

In 1894 an event occurred within the SER that had great significance for its rival, the LCDR; the resignation of Watkin as SER Chairman. Watkin was replaced by three new chairmen in quick succession, none of whom possessed his intolerance and

Gillingham in its South Eastern & Chatham days, with a local stopping train about to pull in (SECR No. 320).

antagonism to the LCDR. They paved the way to better understanding that would ultimately lead to the fusion of the two into one company serving one county, Kent.

The amalgamation was finally achieved in 1899, a convenient date historically, on the very brink of a new age. The resulting joint company took elements of both former parties' names into its new title, the South Eastern & Chatham Railway.

H.S. Wainwright, the initial post-amalgamation CME, from 1899, is the first SECR name to be popularly linked with classes of locomotive that were then a great improvement on the old ones. Among them came the handsome Class C 0-6-0 tender-locomotive of 1900 onwards, a most useful mixed-traffic maid-of-all-work, equally capable of hauling coals or a Continental boat train. Class C functioned well into BR days. Wainwright's Class H 0-4-4T followed in 1904 for the SECR, many of which also worked into the 1950s.

It is instructive to pause at this point and remember the hours worked by railwaymen, in making services possible for their employers, at the turn of the century as compared with today. Ninety per cent of signalmen, pointsmen, switchmen and gatemen worked for twelve hours a day, rarely had a Sunday off, and had only two or three days' holiday a year. Nor did drivers and firemen have much break from duty, working anything from ten

54

Shunting into the extensive freight yards just outside Dover Western docks.

to fifteen hours on an average day; it was not uncommon for them to spend up to eighteen hours on the footplate, with only the occasional Sunday off. Theoretically, platelayers and gangers did better, working a mere ten-hour day with Sundays off 'except for emergency'; but more often than not there *was* some emergency maintenance work to call them out. To become an inspector was thus a worthwhile ambition, with only ten hours a day to work and only a few Sunday rosters.

Old railwaymen, now in their nineties, have recalled to the author how they customarily worked throughout Christmas Day, taking turns to have their own celebrations on Boxing Day, and how they 'worked 365 days a year and never got any holiday' until improving conditions gave them those three precious days. One described how he 'picked up a golden sovereign' (just £1) as his weekly pay as a driver, whereas a porter received only fifteen shillings (75p). Such men appreciated even this improvement after beginning at the bottom as calling-up boys (human alarm clocks equipped with long poles for banging on crewmen's windows to arouse them for early-morning or night rosters). There was thus a very real incentive to work up through the ranks to trainee fireman, fireman, passenger-train fireman, shunter driver, freight driver, suburban driver and finally express driver. But whatever a man's grade, there was true hardship in keeping to his hours at night and before dawn, when no public transport ran; we know of one who habitually cycled all the way from Sidcup to 'The Brick' (Bricklayers Arms depot) for an early turn, thereafter carrying his bicycle laid across the coals on the tender until clocking-off time.

The early 1900s

The locomotive pool following amalgamation consisted, predictably, of old and new, the new being heavier machines packing the sheer strength and power most LCDR engines had lacked. Some of the latter, however, still had at their best some top-class use in them, such as the LCDR Class M 4-4-0s, much used on boat trains.

The Continent, as ever, was the prime passenger target. 'SOUTH EASTERN AND CHATHAM RAILWAY: Royal Mail express services to the CONTINENT via Dover-Folkestone-Queenboro-Calais-Boulogne-Flushing-Ostend. LONDON & PARIS in less than SEVEN HOURS by the Short Sea and Mail routes' ran the company's advertisements of about 1907. Fares offered in connection with the Belgian State Railway & Mail Packet Service, from Dover to Ostend, were boasted as 'the cheapest railway tickets in the world'. Timings were either exaggerated or else superior to our own of today, for the long Dover–Ostend crossing was advertised as taking only three hours, at least half an hour less than it does now.

Before leaving England, these passengers could avail themselves of season tickets on the Belgian railways for their sight-seeing, at only £1 4s 7d (£1.23) First Class, for five days and only 9s 5d (47p) Third. A mere 18s 10d (94p) gave Third Class freedom of the line for a fortnight.

Towards the end of the twentieth century's opening decade, Wainwright brought in his Class P 0-6-0T, a light engine and shunter ideal for working the freight yards of Dover. 1909/10 was a vintage year for Dover, seeing final completion of the docks for Royal Naval as well as merchant shipping use, and the start of work on the splendid-looking new Marine station whose construction was expected to cost no less than £300,000, even at 1910 prices.

Neither the SECR nor its customers, nor its French and Belgian counterparts, were to know that, before the Marine station could be finished, their existence would change dramatically, as the world's most devastating war broke out with unimagined fury.

5
Signal Stop

The last few years leading up to the First World War brought improvements on the SECR whose usefulness was to be short-lived – at least as far as civilian traffic movements were concerned – for they came mainly in the field of Continental services, which one would expect to be destroyed by war.

The luxury trade was further tapped in 1910 with the introduction of the prestigious 60-foot-long Pullman cars on the Charing Cross via Folkestone and the Victoria via Chatham boat-train routes to Dover, bringing a new standard of luxury to the lines. By then, the former had more than come into its own (despite the ever-present bugbear of its longer mileage) until some railwaymen came to consider it the premier route of the two. Shamelessly, the directors here aimed at the upper end of the market.

By excursion to the Continent

As ever, the SECR cashed in on the leading European exhibitions and festivals in its Dover services with such blandishments as: 'The Continent via Dover and Ostend. Three Departures Daily in each direction. Sea passage, Three Hours. SPLENDID TURBINE STEAMERS are running in the service. GHENT Universal and International EXHIBITION under the Patronage of H.M. The King of the Belgians, APRIL TO NOVEMBER 1913.' Special fares were offered, ranging downwards from 44s (£2.20 by today's reckoning) for a cheap excursion from London to Ghent and back, First Class, through a Second Class fare of 28s 6d (£1.42½p) to 18s 6d (92½p) for a spartan Third-Class journey, arriving on the evening of the day of departure from London.

There was little financial limit on how far a passenger could travel in Belgium, for there were on offer 'Cheap Excursion Tickets during the Season to Ostend, Bruges, Ghent, Brussels, Antwerp, Namur and Liège' at about the same cost as a normal single fare. Tickets could be bought in advance in London, or at an agent in Dover, or on the Dover Admiralty Pier itself.

Continental workings apart, SECR coaching stock in general was not exactly distinguished. Ordinary suburban and coastal services tended to be made up of a motley collection of old vehicles left from 'Land 'em Smash 'em and Over' days, including outdated clerestory coaches and a number of excessively small

57

The rolling stock dates this scene to well before the 1923 amalgamation.

baggage vans rattling along behind. There was an element of truth in the exasperated jest that the SECR took more care of its coals than of its human cargoes; for this was the heyday of the Kent Coalfield at Snowdown, as almost all the world ran on coal.

In 1913 only the most far-sighted of seers dreamed of all this ending in a war that would involve the whole nation, and not just troops at the front; the rest of the country went its usual way, patronizing the railways on one hand and perpetually complaining about them on the other. 'THE TRAIN SERVICE: A resolution was received from the Greenwich Council urging all the Borough Councils in the South of London who were served by the South Eastern Railway to take concerted action in memorialising the Board of Trade to compel the SER to modernise their system', ran a typical West Kent newspaper paragraph of that year, followed by the Parliamentary-style comment of (*Laughter*); and undoubtedly there was genuine cause for complaint, as the SECR provided all possible comforts on its Continental trains but herded ordinary passengers into old rolling stock hauled by tired old locomotives, often dating from before the 1899 amalgamation.

Outbreak of war

No part of the United Kingdom stood nearer to France than East Kent, with Dover at the closest point of all. For the railways this

58

Poppy Day collectors at Bromley South station in 1925 with the founder-chairman of the local British Legion branch. This photograph was taken shortly after the advent of Southern Electric.

had previously been only an advantage, creating the boat-train traffic and also a constant movement of cross-Channel freight; but in 1914 the coin was totally reversed. True, Kent in wartime would support a paying new traffic in troop trains, armament trains and hospital trains, but the formerly vital passenger traffic was suddenly gone, literally overnight.

However, work on the new Dover Marine station was not abandoned. On the contrary, its completion was hurried along as an essential part of the wartime transport link; it is thus unique in having been first opened as a naval and military departure point, and only later adapted back for its originally intended civilian use.

As the First World War gathered pace, a great change in women's employment became apparent throughout Britain, but especially in London and south-east England. Railway work was considered vital, 'of national importance', as far as functioning of the trains was concerned; but administrative, office and booking-hall men were soon being drafted into the forces, bound for the Front. So, for the first time in history, women came to work on the lines, taking men's places in booking offices and on platforms. A girl whose previous work had been in a conventional office might well find herself working out long columns of complicated figures in a season-ticket office, battling against time and the timetable to get her finished sheets onto the right train to headquarters.

59

No. 1164 stops at a wayside
station *en route* for Dover.

'For the duration'

Some stations and branches were closed altogether 'for the duration', including Clapham on the final stretch into Victoria,
between Brixton and the terminus and (more surprisingly in view
of the proximity of the Blue Town naval base) part of the line to
Sheerness-on-Sea, one of the oldest parts of the system.

There was naturally no intention of closing the strategically
important old SER approach to Dover via Folkestone and the
Warren, but Mother Nature decreed otherwise; to add to the
problems of the beleaguered SECR, a massive landslide on the
unstable Warren cliffs sent so many tons of earth and chalk onto
the line in 1915 that it had to be closed down for the rest of the war.
Thereafter the former LCDR direct route into Dover was the sole
approach from London.

Railway installations were pressed into all manner of unexpected functions. For instance, the tunnel under Shakespeare

60

Cliff at Dover was used as a ready-made underground store for rail-borne guns, and for trains of armaments and ammunition, which were shunted inside to be completely safe from air raids. This caused no problems to through traffic, for there was none; the tunnel was on the line whose latter course was still blocked by the Warren landslide.

Inevitably, as the railway system geographically closest to the Continental coastline, the SECR shouldered the heaviest burden of war transport work, eternally ferrying troops, supplies and rations down to Chatham, Dover and other ports of embarkation, and bringing back wounded men from the trenches.

More than most ordinary citizens, the company's men came into personal contact with Britain's fighting men, seeing the worst side of their injuries and privations. To them fell the task of running hospital trains from the various Kentish ports, taking wounded men for medical treatment and rehabilitation at inland centres placed as far as possible from the vulnerable coast. The newspapers recorded the front-line heroism and sacrifice in words and imaginative pictures for the population at home, but men working on the SECR often saw the full, unembroidered version of reality, with no niceties attached, as wounded soldiers on crutches limped off ships, groped along half-blinded, or were stretchered onto trains; some had limbs missing, but their faces were full of emotion on first seeing Blighty again.

Seeing such sights, many railwaymen felt compelled to do something extra for the war effort, in a way that would be most appropriate to their own situation, such as joining the St John Ambulance Brigade to acquire a little more expertise in dealing with ambulance trains or with civilian injuries suffered at home in air raids. St John Ambulance recruits were useful to both the army and the railways; they were capable of being seconded in between normal duties to act as stretcher bearers at such points as Chatham naval base, where bad cases were unloaded for road transfer to Fort Pitt Hospital.

Not all these injured men were British Tommies, for some wounded Germans were also brought here; stretcher cases to be unloaded at Fawkham station, between Swanley and Rochester, for onward conveyance to a military hospital in that locality.

Railway workers also found themselves doing extra duties created out of war, such as parcels-office men invoicing and sorting recruits' uniforms and other clothing for the Chatham naval barracks.

Shelling hit Dover in the First as well as the Second World War; at least two railwaymen victims are remembered for the bizarre nature of their deaths; having 'literally had their heads blown off' when leaving a Dover public house. The brilliant gun-flashes of the famous Zeebrugge Raid on Belgium were clearly seen from Dover marshalling yards by men who also witnessed the immortal HMS *Vindictive* drag herself home, reduced virtually to floating

61

Sittingbourne in the early 1900s, with an all-over roof and no footbridge. The waiting train on the left is presumably a connection for Sheerness, standing where its successors still wait today.

scrap iron. And after the war came some macabre cargoes to be handled, including a consignment of regulation military tombstones, along with a shipload of dead French troops being taken home for burial. Wartime on the line was not for the squeamish.

One driver told us how ambulance trains carrying the wounded men brought train crews some little extras as they themselves were almost overloaded with comforts and food from the Red Cross and similar sources; walking through a train, the driver and fireman might well be plied with a tin of dripping here or a leg of lamb there to take home to their wives. We have been given many memories by old Dover railwaymen, among which is recalled a class of locomotive built in Germany but used in Kent, which, reputedly, was never paid for, the First World War breaking out before receipt of the bill.

The unlikeliest ports and the unlikeliest ship

Some unlikely coastal places were selected to become additional ports, created where none had been before, to ease to some extent the growing burden on Dover, Chatham and Sheerness; even remote Richborough on the marshes between Dover and Ramsgate, and modest little Birchington on the north Kent coast, were seriously considered as prospective harbours, never to rival

Most station railings, like these at Chatham, were – if they had survived that long – taken for salvage in the 1940s, and never replaced.

Dover and Chatham but helping to spread their load.

All manner of taxes and impositions were levied to pay for the war effort, not least on the railway line. Well into the years following the Armistice of 1918, supplementary fares were still added to basic travel rates paid by the public; a typical SECR advertisement might thus read: 'CRYSTAL PALACE: Rail, electric trains from Victoria, fifteen minutes' journey. Return fares 1s. 6d., 1s. 2d., 1s. [7½p, 6p and 5p] plus War Supplement'. The Palace itself was closed to the public throughout the war, functioning instead as the biggest 'ship' ever commandeered by the Royal Navy, accommodating thousands of men under the new name of HMS *Crystal Palace* and, at the end of the conflict, staging the biggest demobilization parades in the country as thousands of men were sent back into Civvy Street with the barest minimum of shoes, clothing, and money in their pockets.

Demobbed soldiers poured into HMS *Crystal Palace* until well after the war, as if on a conveyor belt: in one end as troops, out the other as civilians. Train drivers who were active at this period recall demob trains running as late as the first years of Southern electrification by overhead wires, a power source whose dangers were not at first fully appreciated. At least one crewman went down in history for forgetting this where the the wires sagged down low to enter the last High Level Line tunnel. Thoughtlessly standing out of his cab, he brushed the wires, setting his cap and

63

The classic passenger-ferry view of Dover, with the castle outlined on the fast-receding cliffs.

Dover Harbour is on the receding horizon and France lies ahead. This view has scarcely changed since the first boat trains brought cross-Channel passengers down more than a century ago.

hair alight, badly enough to put him into hospital for months.

Wartime or no wartime, the SECR added to its locomotive stable one of the finest and best-looking of its twentieth-century steam engine classes, the handsome 2-6-0 tender locomotive of 1917, the Maunsell Mogul. Its design and functioning were reckoned to be extremely modern and advanced for its day. Many further Moguls were built in the years immediately following the war, and even after the SECR company's second major amalgamation, which put it into the new giant Southern Railway.

The nationwide amalgamation of 1923, which left Britain with just four major railway systems, put an end to the SECR's separate name and existence, carrying it into a new age. War receded ever further back into history and into memory as the heady and happy 1920s brought in the age of the 'Big Four', the named train, and the great European expresses.

6
High Days
and Heady Days

Following fast upon each other came four milestones in Southern Railway history during the 1920s and 1930s: amalgamation, electrification, the first of the great named classes of locomotives, and the introduction or extension of named trains on both Continental and inland routes.

One world war was over and reduced to a commemorative date in the calendar – 11 November – and the next was as yet undreamed of. A 'brave new world' worked hard and played hard, and had better means to enjoy itself than the previous generation: radio, cinema, motoring, electric trains. Travel was cheap and cheerful; a few shillings bought a Cheap Day return ticket to Dover or Margate, and the company in the compartments was cheery and determined to have a good time, despite being jam-packed for up to three hours in a crawling train, with flying 'blacks' or smuts turning their eyes red and watery, and choking smoke turning every tunnel into a sulphurous canyon until the windows were hastily slammed shut.

The luckless suburbanite was still the poor relation when it came to longer-distance travel beyond his own locality, especially on his day outings to the coast, when he was herded like the beast of the field into a crate known as a railway compartment, whose outdated proportions threatened to burst under the pressure of fat mothers, pot-bellied fathers, and swarms of children.

Southern Electric

As early as 1911 it had been written in the popular press: 'The General Manager of the London and Brighton Railway says that estimates are being obtained as to the cost of electrifying the whole main line to Brighton'; but it was the twenties that brought south-eastern electrification, the first nail in the coffin of steam. Electric trains were introduced on the most heavily used suburban lines soon after the 1923 amalgamation, and although the third rail would not extend east of Gillingham until after the Second World War, suburbia itself was almost entirely geared either to this or to the briefly tried overhead-wire system by about 1925–6. The Catford Loop and the main line out of Victoria via Herne Hill were among the earliest Kentish routes to go over to Southern Electric operation, in addition to the so-called Crystal Line from Nunhead

Peckham Rye on the Catford Loop in the earliest days of electrification, with overhead wires instead of the third rail which was later adopted. This photograph was probably taken in about 1925.

up to the Crystal Palace High Level station. Thereafter steam was seen in these regions only for freight and for long-distance Kent Coast and Dover expresses.

In the wake of electrification new schemes continued to bud but never came to fruition, such as a proposed Southern Heights Railway running westwards from Orpington in Kent to Sanderstead in Surrey. This, like the abandoned idea of a line to Eastbourne from Shortlands, was defeated by the hilly and therefore expensive character of the country through which it would have to pass.

In the suburbs travelling conditions were at their worst in the early rush hour before the main rush hour, when workmen's tickets were on sale. As before, the condition of issue was that the holder must finish his journey into London before eight o'clock, which in winter was early dawn. The bait was irresistible to a husband saddled with a mortgage and a young family; a substantial reduction on even the cheapest normal fare encouraged him to join a stampeding herd, all battling at once to reach London with at least one minute to spare.

Workmen's tickets were a godsend financially, but still the battle went on for more flexibility of these and other fares, and in particular for interchange of availability between routes of the same length. 'It would be a great convenience to the public if the return ticket of one company should be available for the other, so

Beckenham Junction. On the right, stands an electric train for Victoria via Crystal Palace, while a steam train runs through from the coast. Electrification was not completed until the 1960s, and this photograph was taken then – in the last days of steam.

that anyone may get out at London Bridge or Charing Cross and return via Victoria or Blackfriars or vice versa. Would not that be a desirable improvement at the present time?' queried a news-paper in the last days of SER and the LCDR; the argument held good after amalgamation, and does to some extent even today.

King Arthur and Lord Nelson

The twenties and thirties saw the building of many of the locomotives which remained kings of Southern steam until the end in the 1960s, which brought into its own the principle of naming a complete class according to some unifying theme. Among these were the majestic 'King Arthur' class of 1925. These magnificent racing machines brought in a new phase of Southern motive power. Their names revived the romance of King Arthur's court, among them *Merlin, Tintagel, Sir Tristram, Sir Launcelot, Sir Galahad, Sir Percivale* and *Sir Agravaine*. It was of a 'King Arthur' class engine that the perceptive explorer of Britain, H.V. Morton, penned the evocative first-hand description 'Sir Percivale' from which we have room for but a few extracts: '"Sir Percivale" comes thundering up through Kent, the night Continental boat train behind him, his lean, lithe one hundred and twenty-nine tons flung out over the track like a running leopard. . . The line of his lit Pullman cars is like a string of pearls

Bickley as few local people can remember it.

flashed through the hop-fields, whipped through the night against the Pilgrims' Way; and he comes so regularly, and goes so swifty, that only the newest born rabbits at the edge of the woods dream of showing their little tails at him. He is not as heavy as the "Caerphilly Castle" or as famous as the "Flying Scotsman" but, to me, he is a poem in steel, for, in the roar of his wheels, if you know him well, is the most lovely song in all the world. . . . He stands in Victoria covered with the sweat of his run, his six-foot-seven driving wheels moist with green oil, his great connecting and side rods silver with effort, his pistons bright, the flanges of his bogie wheels white as new shillings. . . . A squat little shunter departs with the Pullman cars; and "Sir Percivale", with a mighty snort and a puff of sudden steam, backs his long leanness out of Victoria into that place where all engines go at night to be fussed and washed and patted and bathed and made ready for new miles.'

On the heels of the 'King Arthur' class followed, in 1926, Maunsell's closely related 'Lord Nelson' class, a locomotive of over 83 tons with a tender of some 57 tons. Again, a theme bound the class together, with stirring names of the sea.

Sunny South Express

Even holiday trains often had names as a distinction, notably the *Sunny South Expresses*, roaring into Kent under steam bringing loads of 'foreigners' from other railway systems into Southern territory for the day. To those interested in trains they were worth watching for, in case the *Sunny South* should have brought its own engine, from the GWR or the LMS. These were the only times most southerners would ever set eyes on the sleek greyhounds of the GWR, gleaming with brass and Brunswick green, or the massive machines of the LMS or LNER.

The Southern brought in the 'South for Sunshine' campaign, for publicizing as 'the finest resorts in the world' such destinations as Folkestone, Deal, Dover (then truly a resort and not just, as it is today, mainly a port), Hythe and Sandgate. The company had its own hotel, the South Eastern, at Deal, not far from Dover, 'within reach of the Four Famous Golf Links: Royal Cinque Ports, Prince's, Walmer & Kingsdown, Royal St. George's'. On the line it offered weekend tickets all year round, with eight- and fifteen-day tourist tickets in summer. For another sixpence ($2\frac{1}{2}$p) the railway company would supply its *Hints for Holidays*, six hundred pages of text and hotel advertisements. Also over part of the Dover line, as far as Faversham where it joined the north Kent coast route, ran the *Thanet Pullman* or *Thanet Pullman Limited*, continued by the Southern from SECR days.

Still concentrating on the Continent and its approaches through Dover, rather than on the metals between Dover and suburbia, the Southern Railway followed the completion of Dover Marine station by rebuilding the companion Priory station about a mile inland, serving the town as well as the landward approaches to both the Eastern and Western docks. A new motive-power depot was also opened, nearer to the Marine station.

Second Class Abolished

Second Class travel was generally abandoned in about 1923 but, as ever, the customer travelling onwards from Dover received special consideration; for him, seated in his well-founded express, Second Class was retained as an alternative in terms of cash to the rigours of Third or the expense of First; on these trains, some Second Class accommodation was offered beyond the years of the Second World War.

The Continental passenger was wooed with ever-improving conditions, more and more prestigious carriages, and increasingly powerful engines. Still more elegant Continental coaches were introduced in 1921 – broad, airy and dignified, setting a new standard for the Southern. Even certain locomotive classes were rostered to these trains in preference to doing run-of-the-mill trips for Everyman, among them the rebuilt E1 and D1 classes. New and faster ferries were also built for connecting the British and French halves of these services, such as the *Isle of Thanet* and the *Maid of Kent*, carrying the Kentish theme into European waters. In 1925 improved arrangements were made with the

An engine runs light to the watering tower at busy Chatham, a naval base and port, as well as an important station *en route* to Dover.

Belgian State Railways for better timings on the main Dover–Ostend services.

The Orient-Express

Railway romance was surely never more headily present than in the *Orient-Express* in its twenties heyday; a train whose origins went back to the respectable antiquity of 1883 (the *Orient-Express*) and 1906 (the extended *Simplon-Orient-Express*, with through carriages to Belgrade, Sofia and Constantinople, now Istanbul). From its 1883 inauguration it set new standards of luxury and refinement, offering gracious living in the confined space of a railway saloon, when one dressed for dinner as if in the best hotels. It was just Not Done to wear the same dress twice, or the same outfit for dinner as was worn for lunch, which meant mountains of luggage for the train's lady patrons. The original *Express* carried only about forty passengers, who spent three nights on board once the run was fully extended across Bulgaria to Constantinople.

The 'Train of Kings', or alternatively the 'King of Trains', was the gateway to Europe's most elegant capitals: Paris, Vienna, Budapest and Bucharest.

During the 1920s the *Simplon-Orient-Express* truly came into its

71

The deserted appearance of a station was characteristic of steam days in Kent; yet the three railwaymen's uniforms have a strangely modern look, similar to the striped-sleeved jackets issued by BR in the 1970s.

own, when the Simplon Tunnel under the Alps was completed by a second bore, bringing Paris (and London, through the British connecting express) nearer than ever before to Venice and the mysterious Balkans. Between the two world wars it was Europe's most exclusive service; even war brought some glory (although the train itself could not run), for it was aboard one of its Wagons-Lits cars that the German surrender was signed in 1918. In the twenties it regained or even surpassed its old character, although for a time Germany and Austria were avoided on the journey, and the train was routed instead through Lausanne, Brigue, the Simplon Tunnel, Venice, Trieste and Belgrade. From 1921 it ran the full route again, taking only fifty-six hours from Paris, a record speed that seems never to have been bettered. Rich Britons patronized mainly the Calais to Paris section, travelling via Dover and the Channel steamer to join the main European part of the train; others went farther afield: officials and their families on the way to and from diplomatic appointments; oilmen travelling to Iraq and the Persian Gulf; wealthy sightseers doing the Grand Tour because it was the Done Thing; others bound for Egypt, one of the most fashionable countries; some going to Venice where they could afford to rent an entire palazzo for the season.

Bulgaria provided a contact with royalty which the more nervous passengers could well have done without, when King Boris III of that country elected to follow his personal railway

Kearsney has a clean, functional and modern look in this photograph – until the lack of a third rail betrays its age.

mania by going onto the footplate and taking over the controls. The King was sufficiently recognized as an engine driver to have once been allowed, in Britain, to drive the *Royal Scot* from London to Crewe, albeit with a qualified inspector with him. In his own country, as monarch, he could take over virtually any train he chose, including the *Orient*, and drive it in his own fashion, at his own breakneck speed. At Sofia he would board the *Orient-Express* and assume command of it and its passengers, pushing the engine to the limit of its working capacity in a way that appalled the crew, who dared not protest. An occasion in 1934 is particularly well remembered, when King Boris was for once acting as fireman. When a firebox blowback severely injured the driver, the King took charge, drove on to the next station of importance, saw the injured man to hospital, and climbed straight back onto the footplate. Without even waiting for a new driver he roared off to the frontier, careering along at 70 miles an hour (when 60 mph was reckoned to be the safe maximum), there to hand the train over to the next scheduled crew.

Murder on the Orient Express

It was around the Paris–Vienna section of this famous train that literature and the cinema wove sagas of mystery and intrigue, inspired by the train's real-life complement of royalty, riches, high

73

'Down' slow train from Victoria on the alternative ex-SER route to Dover. This photograph shows an E class 4-4-0 locomotive, No. A157, passing through Knockholt in 1928.

position and aristocracy, cooped up together for three days and nights aboard this aristocrat of the railway world. Ironically, the best known of them all, Agatha Christie's *Murder on the Orient Express*, was not originally known by that title, but was first called *Murder in the Calais Coach*. At least one of the book's scenes was fact as well as fiction; the particularly vicious snowstorm which marooned the train on the line for three days did actually happen, in the cruel winter of 1929; not on the northern or alpine sections of the line (as might be expected in winter) but almost as far south as it ran, near the Turkish border. The train was stranded for three days, and its passengers lived not on exotic cuisine but on such iron rations as the crew could obtain by struggling through deep snowdrifts to the nearest village. This was the only time that the *Orient* suffered delay of any real note.

A total of six films, about twenty books, and an 'Orient-Express Foxtrot' conspired with fact and rumour to glamorize the *Orient-Express* and, in its reflected glory, the Continental expresses which ferried its British contingent down to Dover.

Some of the splendid golden Pullman cars forming the modern revived *Venice-Simplon-Orient-Express* on the London to the Kentish port part of its run, were built at about this time, including *Ibis* (1925), which was sold to the Wagons-Lits Company and initially saw service in Italy; *Rainbow* (now *Phoenix*) burned out in 1936 but later restored; *Zena*, which served on the *Bournemouth Belle* in the late twenties; and *Minerva* of 1927.

Fast sea crossings

Businessmen as well as society people used the *Orient-Express*. Lesser commercial voyagers were, by the early twenties, going to the Continent by various *Short Sea Route Expresses* in sufficient numbers for the railways openly to woo them as a source of revenue. The SECR's pre-amalgamation advertisement was still being repeated in guidebooks of 1923-4: 'For European Business journeys . . . travel by the SHORT SEA ROUTE to the CONTINENT'. As before the First World War, the company's timings were either superior to our own modern ones, or else an embellishment for attracting custom, for these advertisements spoke of 'Dover–Calais: Folkestone–Boulogne, duration of Sea Passage 60m : 80m' (75 minutes and 90 minutes are the respective minima today). Dover–Ostend was again offered at only three hours (3½ hours or more today, except by Jetfoil); and Folkestone–Flushing in five hours (a service which no longer exists; the only comparable crossing, from Sheerness to Flushing, now takes about seven hours).

1929 was a vintage year for the Continental workings of the Southern, when its most famous and prestigious boat train was put

The biggest pub sign in Beckenham: top part of a genuine signal gantry forming the sign for the Golden Arrow opposite Beckenham Junction station, through which the *Arrow* passed daily. There is another Golden Arrow pub at Dover.

Dover Docks seen here in the early 1920s, with two old-fashioned ferries in view. The condition of the wooden planking and railings leaves something to be desired.

into service, the *Golden Arrow*, the inaugural run of which was staged in May. Perhaps only the *Flying Scotsman* exerted a greater pull on the ordinary public than this magnificent-looking rake of all-Pullman coaches, sumptuously fitted within and aristo-cratically decorated without, a flash of gold which, by both its colouring and its speed, justified the train's title.

As for the post-war *Arrow*, a special group of engines was specially maintained in racing condition for working this flagship service; the *Golden Arrow* could never be allowed to break down.

Arrow passengers initially had their own ferry, with special luxury accommodation for the Channel crossing which took them to join the French portion of the train, the *Flèche d'Or*. The ship was the *Canterbury*, later rearranged to carry both *Golden Arrow* and ordinary Continental passengers on other *Short Sea Route* departures from Dover. The *Canterbury* cost over £200,000, even in 1920, and was notable for her roominess and air of luxury; fittings were of high quality and elegance, and the ship boasted a Palm Court in the landborne Grand Hotel manner. She carried only about three hundred passengers when full, free of the milling about of lost-sheep travellers which is still the chief drawback of a Channel crossing. *Golden Arrow* passengers are said even to have had special Customs clearance, avoiding the workaday hustle and

77

An elegant steamer of a type often seen at Dover in the 1920s.

bustle of a busy port, one of several factors intended to attract the sort of well-heeled passenger who would today travel First Class by air. Overcrowding on the *Golden Arrow* itself was impossible, as all seats were numbered and reserved as part of the service. Wealthy travellers used the *Golden Arrow* as their feeder service to the *Orient-Express* via Boulogne or Calais.

The Victoria Station morning departure of the *Arrow* was a ritual, again comparable to that of the *Flying Scotsman* in its sacrosanct formality. Its timing was exact; exactly 98 minutes from Victoria to the port, almost the same as today's boat-train runs, and departure was always expected to be on time; if the 'Arrer' (as south Londoners called it) ran more than a few minutes late, something serious must have happened. Between London and Paris, including crossing the Channel, the total journey time was only $6\frac{1}{2}$ hours; a timing hard to beat even today. Watching the train shoot past was, like the London departure, a ritual for people living near the main line. All year round, families who cared nothing for any other train would congregate on foot-bridges and road-bridges throughout the suburbs to watch the famous train tear past in a hiss of steam and a flash of gilded arrows. There was barely time to take in the elaborately decorated Pullmans, the distinctive red-shaded table-lamps, and the faces of the privileged at the windows, before the train was gone – as literal an illustration of a shot from a marksman's bow as could possibly be achieved on rails. Later, in its inter-war period, the *Arrow* temporarily lost something of this prestige and atmosphere when, in the 1930s, the all-Pullman image was diminished and the Second Class Pullmans were replaced by ordinary express carriages which were hardly as glamorous.

Another Maunsell class, of new 4-4-0 locomotives, was introduced in 1930, the handsome 'Schools' class whose names are still affectionately remembered from their latter working days into the 1950s and early 1960s: *Cheltenham, Repton, Hurstpierpoint, Christ's Hospital*, and many others. They were among the last new engines commissioned before the Southern broke away from tradition in external appearance with the streamlined Bulleid Pacifics, and were believed to be the most powerful 4-4-0 engines in Europe; they became very popular with drivers for their easy handling, and were capable (unofficially) of touching 90 miles an hour on favourable stretches of track.

Varied traffic

The late twenties and early thirties saw the greatest outbreak of suburban building since Victorian times. Large areas of lovely countryside vanished under interminable spreads of all-alike new avenues and crescents, as far out of London as Orpington and Petts Wood. 'They'll never sell them at *that* price!' people scoffed about £900 Petts Wood stockbroker-belt houses, when £600–£700 was the average cost of a house; but they did sell, and many more besides, bringing a surge of new custom to local stations as the men from the new estates flocked up to London to earn the wherewithal to pay off their mortgages. Often on the West Kent lines, one, two or even three new footbridges would spring up across the railway, sometimes quite close together, leading to nothing but open fields; they were a sure sign that the houses would follow, and quickly. Railways were the principal method for all these people to get around their newly developed neighbourhood, for cars were so few as to seem unlikely ever to rival trains. To quote but one typical commentator of the mid-twenties: 'Even the motor car, wonderful invention that it undoubtedly is, cannot take the place of the railway. How long would our highways bear up against the ceaseless traffic involved in bringing London's coals from the coalfields by road, to mention only one bulky and heavy commodity used in every house? How could the vast population of London get to and from work by road, even with motor-cars and buses, if it were not for the fine system of steam and electric railways, which spread out like a spider's web from the city's heart to the distant suburbs?'

Bromley South as nobody under the age of about sixty can remember it; the milk churns on the platform were from farms where there are now miles of suburbia.

Few people had any reason to imagine that this world of peace, whose main worry was the Depression, would ever change into a nightmare, as it had changed once before, a mere quarter of a century earlier; or even that the local progress of railway electrification would be halted for the same reason. In 1935 the

Once a footbridge to nowhere. Local people were puzzled when bridges like this were built over the Dover line leading only to open fields. The housing estates that quickly grew up explained the seemingly pointless footbridges.

Even in suburbia there are signs of the past: an unelectrified section of track and two discarded sets of wheels from a linesman's trolley.

third rail was continued from Orpington through to Sevenoaks and, on the Dover line, from Bickley through to Swanley, whence the other route down to Sevenoaks was also converted. Aiming for the coast, it reached out again from Swanley, eastwards, as far as Gillingham, which was to remain as its final destination until about twenty years later, after another war had taken its course, together with the lean years of austerity which immediately followed it. Until then, steam would still be master on journeys of any real distance.

New docks approaches were added in the Dover Admiralty Pier area, for easier loading and unloading of train ferries going directly into Europe. With their completion, a new direct service to Paris by night was inaugurated, known to the general public (on account of its richly liveried Wagons-Lits) as the 'Blue Train'. In London there was even a Blue Train Restaurant, which quickly became known as a fashionable society rendezvous.

However, the average passenger would never set foot in Paris. Apart from workday journeys, his travels were made up mainly of family outings to the seaside. In the thirties, for a mere five shillings (25p) he could go from Bickley or Bromley all the way to the Kent coast, and his children could travel for half that modest fare. On a fine Saturday or Sunday morning, or on a Bank Holiday, it was common for the ticket queue to stretch out of Bromley South station, through the forecourt and into the High Street. When at last a family received their tickets and trooped downstairs to the platform, they often found that the train had arrived already so overcrowded that it proved literally impossible to force their way in for standing room. Even the modern rush hour pales by comparison with a slow steam train so jam-packed that thirty people were crammed into the guard's van, more than that in each luggage van. Those able to squeeze into the corridors were so hemmed in that the people on the outside were forced to push their heads and shoulders out of the open windows, unable even to stand upright. These passengers were the worst affected in tunnels; they were smothered in smuts, coughing and spluttering, and found it difficult to move their elbows sufficiently to reach the leather straps which controlled the windows, to slam them shut and fasten the straps over the big brass studs. In damp weather, or if rain threatened, even the lucky passengers *seated* by the windows could see nothing of the countryside, only the swirls of foggy white vapour which today's steam-hungry enthusiast calls romantic; the reality was simply infuriating and frustrating.

At journey's end, both going out and coming home, it was customary for a mother to take her children, cowering against the noise of escaping steam and the sheer pulsating heat, up to the engine and to thank the driver for a safe journey. Even adults often thanked the driver, a courtesy which somehow never occurs to us on leaving an electric train.

At this period the old-fashioned technique of slip-coaches was

Cygnus and *Perseus*, two of the luxurious Pullman cars fully restored for the revived *Orient-Express*. *Cygnus* ran on the *Golden Arrow*'s last journey; *Perseus* also formed part of the *Golden Arrow* rake, and was used for Sir Winston Churchill's funeral train.

still practised on the route to Dover via Folkestone, as when the one o'clock train from Charing Cross slipped one or more coaches for Ashford, thus eliminating the delay of a stop there.

Hop-pickers' specials remained up to the very brink of war a regular feature of railway life. In its last issue before the outbreak of hostilities in September 1939, the *Kentish Times* reported that hoppers still went about their peacetime working holidays, but carried with them the appurtenances of an approaching holocaust: 'HOP PICKERS INVADE KENT. . . . A special train carrying hundreds of hop-pickers from the East End of London left London Bridge station for the Kent hop gardens early on Tuesday morning. The general exodus of pickers, however, is not expected to begin until Thursday or Friday.' That general exodus would, as usual, include trains bound for the Faversham, Dover and Folkestone lines; or rather for the farms and villages on them. This report continued: 'All arrangements are ready for the special trains to start running, and the majority of pickers will receive their cards, notifying them that their services are needed, within the next few days. They have been advised by the Home Office to take their gas masks with them. Many of the 100,000 pickers required to harvest this year's crop will travel to the gardens in cars, motor coaches and lorries. It is estimated that each family of

pickers can earn from £10 to £15 during the three weeks. Last year Kent produced 150,300 cwt of hops, out of Britain's total production of 257,000 cwt and this year a crop of finer quality is anticipated. The past fortnight of almost continuous sunshine will mean much to the quality of next year's beer; it has ripened the bines very quickly, and the crop will be heavier than last year. . . Excellent accommodation will be provided for the pickers in Kent. There will be large car parks for the cars of pickers and their visitors, and improved two-storey huts have been erected.'

Thus we have two portents in one short report: the nearness of war, reflected in the order to carry gas masks; and the emergence of the car as a rival to the train which, once the war was over, would inflict wounds on the railway as supreme carrier that only the busiest main lines would survive.

Right up to the brink of the war, through that last glowing

83

summer, the usual succession of Sunday School outings and works outings by train continued, for such parties almost invariably travelled by rail in specially reserved coaches, over any distance beyond their own localities (which were tackled by bus or charabanc). Specials were sometimes chartered complete, or a set of reserved carriages was attached to a normal service, aiming at the Kent Coast via Faversham and therefore travelling for about three-quarters of the way along the Dover route. Some even aimed as far afield as Boulogne or Calais, out of Folkestone or Dover. Wherever they were bound, the order of the day during the journey down was to sing hymns and popular songs, accompanied by a passenger with a squeeze-box accordion, and most of the way back as well, creating a happy pandemonium on the move. Under steam, it could take about three wearisome hours to reach the sea, so that passengers often arrived only in time for lunch, and then had to leave again at tea time.

One particular coastal trip was never forgotten by the author's parents and grandparents: the journey home one late summer evening of 1939, only days before the declaration of war. From the train they could see the sun setting behind a darkening landscape of Kentish orchards in a way that even the most unobservant passenger could not fail to notice; a great crimson orb on the horizon and the sky streaked as if with blood. 'It seems like an omen, dears,' said Granny. And it was.

7
The Front Line

In the centre of the seafront at Dover today there stands a deteriorating glass-covered chart commemorating the Second World War shelling of the town and port from across the Channel. Each month of that long period is represented by an evil-looking grey Nazi shell painted with a number – the tally of shells homing on target during that month. To look at it is to realize that more than one miracle of the war affected this town; not only that of Dunkirk, but also the near-miracle that Dover is still there at all, especially its famous castle, perched so vulnerably on the cliff top like the apple on the head of William Tell's son. It seems impossible that such a prominent landmark could have survived so savage an onslaught spread over so many months.

Dover today is everywhere punctuated by modern buildings which fill in gaps where destruction ate away the old terraces and shopping streets, and a church under the castle cliff remains in ruins as the shelling left it, a visible reminder of war's tragedy. And yet so much that is historic somehow survives, its repaired wounds so well blended in by passing time that they are often difficult to detect. On the spider's web of railways and sidings spreading between the Priory and Western Docks stations and into the docks area, it is similarly hard now to identify exactly where they were bombed and shelled night after night. Few areas outside the big cities suffered more than Dover, which faced directly the Nazi-occupied coast of France; and few rail systems were forced to cope with greater strains on their resources while at the same time sharing in the general destruction.

Evacuation by train

Everyone who knew the Southern Railway in wartime, whether as passenger or crew, acquired his own fund of outstanding memories. For some it is the war's opening days that stand out most vividly; the period of evacuee trains bringing London children out of the capital by thousands, into a supposedly safe seaside and country area (which proved, in fact, to be anything but safe). Such a mass movement of child passengers, accomplished in only three or four days, had never been undertaken before, and the Southern therefore had no comparable experience upon which to draw. At the same time the company was expected to cope with

85

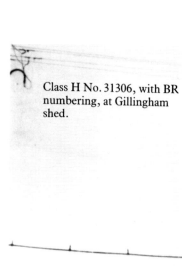

Class H No. 31306, with BR
numbering, at Gillingham
shed.

Class L 1770 at Ashford. This photograph was taken in 1947, the year before nationalization; the livery is therefore in SR's malachite green. Class L locomotives were much used on local semi-fast passenger workings in Kent.

mass transport of another kind: of goods, supplies and all manner of wartime freight. Yet, though stretched beyond all normal limits, the Southern managed to move tens of thousands of schoolchildren out of London within a few days of war being officially declared. Somehow rolling stock was produced out of the proverbial hat. Fleets of buses materialized to ferry whole schools to the London termini and, at journey's end, onwards to commandeered schools and halls where the harrowing business of billeting could begin. Perhaps more than anything else, the evacuee trains brought home to Londoners the fact that they were at war with a foreign power, as they watched thousands of young pupils converging at the stations; each child carried a gas mask in an oblong cardboard box slung by string around his or her neck, and was labelled with his name, like a lost puppy waiting to be claimed. In an endless succession of crocodiles, two by two, they marched from their school assembly-points to join these buses and trains bound for 'Somewhere in Kent'. On arrival the children were formed up again for their first steps into a bewildering new life; they were foisted upon sometimes unwilling strangers, and were far from home and without their parents, often for the first time. Teams of volunteers met each incoming train; they wore identifyir.g armbands and badges, and relieved the railway of further responsibility by sorting out the mêlée on the platform into bus loads. Each bus was bound for a different billeting point. Some evacuee trains halted at several stations *en route*, to disgorge

A perky little Wainwright 0-6-0 Class C topping the bank out of Chatham Dockyard towards Gillingham. This was a class used on local passenger services, such as the shuttle needed after a flying-bomb had hit the line near Newington.

one or more carriage loads at each, before going on with the rest to the next disembarkation point. During the first days of September 1939, the Southern provided over two hundred special trains – seventy or more a day. Curiously, not all of them were packed to capacity, for there were always some families who elected, at the last moment, to stay behind with familiar things and places, and risk their lives for the sake of home.

The Medway Towns (Rochester, Rainham, Chatham, Gillingham and Strood) witnessed their own mass exodus by another series of evacuee specials, as these towns were recogized as dangerous points because of the proximity, as legitimate war targets, of Chatham dockyard and the Medway shipping. Initially the children from the Medway Towns were sent no farther away than other parts of their own county, in the mistaken belief that rural Kent would be safer than urban Chatham; the probability that the French coast might be occupied and used as a springboard to England was not as yet appreciated. More than fifty specials pulled out of the Medway Towns carrying over 35,000 passengers, including teachers and helpers from this heavily built-up area. Even the remand home in the village of Borstal (from which similar homes elsewhere took their name) had to be evacuated of its mainly youthful inhabitants.

Another thirteen chartered trains brought evacuees from the north Kent industrial waterfront on the Thames into the county's more rural quarters, since it was quickly realized that the heavy

The former engine-shed at Bromley South. Although not used for locomotives for about four decades, it still survives in commercial use.

riverside industries would attract enemy bombers.

Evacuation was a sight that witnesses do not readily forget; the first public exhibition of war's reality, tearing countless families apart for the children's sake. Hour after hour those two-by-two crocodiles tramped through the streets to their nearest stations and bus stops; tiny sisters and ostentatiously brave bigger brothers holding hands; some excited, others tearful and fearful. The total number of children evacuated from London was more than a million, many of them bound for Kent.

Birth of the blackout

The next inescapable demonstration that Britain was at war was the blackout. The world was suddenly dark; not with the darkness of a normal night, punctuated by friendly pinpoints of light from streets and stations and houses, but with the inky all-enveloping blackness of a world before artificial light was invented. Suddenly, one of the most sought-after commodities was the humble electric torch, and batteries sold in millions. Shops did a roaring trade in thick, heavy, black fabric for making blackout curtains. Fathers spent their evenings nailing together shutters of cardboard and plywood for fitting inside their windows before drawing the curtains and switching on a light – for even the best curtains were not good enough if one tiny chink of light

90

This is now only seen on sidings within the wholly electrified Dover route; standard track without the third rail.

existed at their edges to attract a thunderous thumping at the door from a vigilant policeman or air-raid warden. Familiar scenes seemed alien as people groped their way by tiny torch beams, and catching a train after dark was at first such a nightmare experience that nobody travelled unless it was vital to do so.

Total blackness enveloped the average station in the first weeks of the war, with nothing to give even the faintest sense of direction unless there was a moon. A passenger's first hazard was the platform edge, as he inched along in fear of going too near and falling onto the track. Later, white lines were painted as reflectors. It was almost impossible to identify the waiting-room or the ladies' room, for none of the usual signs could be read, and the windows were blacked out from inside. When the train pulled in, it was in pitch darkness. Was a compartment full or half empty? The only way to find out was to get in and grope blindly for a seat along a line of rigidly resisting knees. Disembodied grunts and growls of 'Do you mind?' came out of the darkness as a newly arrived passenger unavoidably touched portions of anatomy, apologizing to each voice along the row until his hand at last touched railway-company upholstery and a seat. The only way to ensure alighting at the right station instead of some unilluminated halt was to memorize the order of all the stops on the journey, counting them off one by one, for every platform was in darkness and the booking hall was blacked out. It was only a porter's shout that saved many a traveller from being stranded on the wrong country station,

91

Dover Priory (formerly Dover Town) where trains run in via a short tunnel which was used as a wartime shelter for rolling stock during air raids.

perhaps with hours to wait for the next train. In time a variety of safety lighting was evolved, supposedly invisible from the air, which was allowed to be used with police permission. It was so dim as to be useless by normal standards, but better by far than no light at all. All station lamps had to be painted or sprayed with a thick blue paint, reducing the light from a normal electric bulb or gas-mantle to a ghostly flicker, which must be instantly extinguished on notification of any air-raid warning. Again, it was impossible to read a book or newspaper to render the journey less tedious, but at least a vacant seat could be found without difficulty. A type of white light was eventually allowed in carriages provided that their windows were totally blacked out with blinds. This light was to be turned out at a central switch on the train on receipt of a warning by a specially appointed lighting warden. His duty was to snuff out the white lamps and replace them with dim blue ones during an alert, and to check and re-check that all window blinds were fully down and closely fitted as dusk approached.

The blackout continued

During the hours of night, the lighting attendant paced the train corridors, checking that no window was accidentally left uncovered, and that no blind's light-tightness was disturbed when a

Dover summed up in one picture: the White Cliffs, ships, cranes, sheds and railway lines. The photograph was taken from the road into Western Docks Station.

door was opened as a passenger got out.

In a small claustrophobic compartment after dark, with every chink of ventilation shut out along with the outside world, the atmosphere was unwholesome in the extreme.

However, one thing could not be blacked out – the metals themselves. The more intensively they were used, the better they were as geographical guidelines, leading raiding bombers to big cities and railway targets. Nearer to London, the tracks were more heavily used, and therefore shinier and better as landmarks; a vicious circle, responsible for many an onslaught on a junction or marshalling yard.

Iron and steel fixtures and fittings of all kinds suddenly disappeared from the urban scene; by official order they were chopped off and taken away for a use vaguely known as 'munitions'. Station forecourts everywhere lost their spiked railings (which in many cases were never replaced) leaving only a row of inch-high jagged stumps along the top of the supporting wall, looking like docked tails at a dog show.

Everything that could be a clue to a potential invader as to his whereabouts was ruthlessly eradicated, making any town a puzzle to visitors. Teams of workmen went around the lanes and streets of Kent, as elsewhere, setting ladders against signposts and blacking out with thick paint the name of every town and village. Names of parishes were painted out of church notice boards and,

93

The Southern as German air crews liked to see it : almost dark, with the last light showing up the shiny rails as streaks of silver which no blackout could hide. The lines were the raiders' directional signs into London and other target cities.

of course, the names of stations. The most that was left was the legend '—— North', or 'South ——' or the useless '——-on-Sea'.

Troop trains and armoured trains

Trains such as most lineside residents had never seen before rumbled past their back gardens, ranging from special armoured trains (which included one constructed at Ashford and based at Canterbury) to troop trains bound for camps and transit points – long lines of peacetime Southern rolling stock packed with boys in khaki instead of children bound for the seaside. They sang to keep up their spirits as they went, or hung out of the windows, whistling at every girl in sight and catcalling along the train in the pretence that this was a pleasure trip instead of the first stage of a journey leading to probable death. Those who did survive went down this line as boys, and came back as men. Innumerable troop trains passed through the busy junction of Faversham, where the Dover and Ramsgate lines diverged, sometimes stopping there to water the engine – often a 'Lord Nelson' class locomotive still in its pre-war Southern livery.

94

Dunkirk

Dunkirk in 1940 affected Dover in many ways. In common with ports and resorts all around the Kent coastline, Dover gave its 'little ships' to the historic evacuation: peacetime pleasure launches, old paddle steamers, fishing boats, river craft. They came back packed to their limits with exhausted and dirty troops whose only possessions were their rifles and the muddy uniforms they stood up in. Secondly, it was Dover (together with its sister ports of Folkestone, Sheerness and Ramsgate) which organized their onward despatch from the quays to the railheads, and from there to inland reception camps and family reunions. The precision with which the Southern Railway took over thousands upon thousands of incoming men and found trains for them was in itself akin to a military exercise.

Between the end of May and the first weekend of June 1940, train followed train out of the ports, packed with young men experiencing the wonder of being safely back in Blighty. The principal problem was to assemble enough coaches to accommodate this seemingly interminable stream of troops, a problem which the other three main railways – LNER, GWR and LMS – helped to solve by sending in over a hundred extra trains to Kent, Sussex (Newhaven) and Hampshire (Southampton), to back up the Southern's own fifty-five specials, most of them working out of Dover, Folkestone, Sheerness, Margate and Ramsgate. Dover inevitably bore the brunt, seeing no less than 327 troop trains out

The spider's web of tracks and points where the Dover and Ramsgate lines diverge at Faversham, once one of the Southern's most busy sheds. As a busy junction, it was much raided during the war.

The majesty of the 'Lord Nelson' class. An 'up' Continental boat train leaving Dover Marine in 1939, just before the outbreak of war, hauled by No. 856 *Lord St Vincent*.

in about ten days of frantic activity. Sometimes as many as fifty or sixty ships, of all possible sizes and tonnages, lay alongside Dover's many quays at one time, carrying back anything from a hundred to over a thousand weary men. Empty rolling stock poured in from all directions, was quickly turned round and sent back for another load of survivors; some trains had to be held back at various inland points until clearance was given to move them in again. And still it seemed that for every thousand men sent on their way another two thousand came in (which was probably true).

Fighting their way along the platforms went teams of volunteers, handing cups of tea through open carriage windows, together with other simple comforts and cigarettes. The best cup of tea a man had ever tasted was gulped from a tin mug on Dover station.

Witnesses along the line still vividly remember this constant procession of troop trains taking British and Allied survivors of Dunkirk to inland reception camps, pouring through Chatham and Rochester on their way to London. It is said that over 300,000 men came through Dover alone in the aftermath of Dunkirk.

The terror by shelling

Ordeal by bombs and blitz was the lot of every town in the southeast, but Dover suffered an additional terror which was confined to that part of the Kent coast which lay within range of occupied France, whose cliffs could clearly be seen in the distance in fine weather. Conversely, Dover and Folkestone could be seen from Cap Gris-Nez, perfect targets for long-range shells shot with deadly accuracy across twenty-one miles of water to land with even greater destructive power than ordinary bombs. Not for nothing was this quarter of Kent nicknamed Hell Fire Corner.

The shelling of Dover lasted intermittently for four years, but its greatest savagery was concentrated into 1941–2. To escape with their lives, if not their possessions, many residents emulated those who sheltered in the more famous Chislehurst Caves by moving into the numerous chalk caverns in their own legendary White Cliffs. Railwaymen could not retreat during duty hours, but had to carry on alongside firemen and policemen, all workers in the public interest. For off-duty moments when retreat was possible, however, Dover crews shovelled out their own dugouts from the chalky bluffs beside the line between Dover Town and Marine. Those in the docks area, within sight of the Channel, learned to recognize the telltale flash of a shell being fired from Calais, and to calculate exactly how long it would take to cross the Channel: just 53 seconds; time enough to scramble off a goods wagon and crawl underneath it, or to get behind one of the innumerable concrete tank-traps that were erected wherever there was a railway target. Over five hundred shells landed on Dover town and port, causing great destruction, while up to four

The network of tracks and points at Dover.

thousand homed on its hinterland. More than two hundred people were killed, and many others wounded and made homeless. Even the famous Romney Marsh sheep had to be evacuated as possible invasion victims; they were moved by rail to new pastures inland, away from their open marshes which swept right down to the Channel battlefront.

Railwaymen's memories of war

If Dover's caves were a godsend to sheltering civilians, its man-made tunnels were equally valuable to the railways. It was impossible to enter Priory station without going through one of the tunnels flanking it on either side, rendering this stretch an ideal air-raid shelter for valuable rolling stock, which could be shunted inside when shelling or bombing began. Passengers caught outside in a raid tended to follow suit, like rabbits making for a convenient burrow, congregating in the dark tunnels as the earth shook with shells thudding into what was left of their town.

To talk to the railwaymen of Dover and other Kent towns is to feel, as if at first hand, the purely human aspect of a life made up of mirthless austerity, under a rain of bombs and shells, when work had somehow to continue. Each man has his own particular memories. A former driver described to the author how crews took their rationed meals with them to eat on the footplate, never having any real idea of when or how they might reach home after work, when rails were being constantly blown up and buckled. More than one railwayman remembered doing a nineteen-hour turn of duty, when raids made it impossible to return to base and

99

Southern No. 1727 coasts into Dover Priory.

home. Tired and hungry, all some crews could find for sustenance was a helping of toast at a café which miraculously was found to be open; 'the loveliest piece of toast I ever had', as one driver recalled. It is said that railwaymen were among those classified as workers 'of national importance' and were granted a tiny additional ration of certain basic foods to enable them to tackle their gruelling hours and duties – a few pitiful ounces more of cheese, sugar and tea. On night duty, with raids at their height, they were always uncertain when they might get a proper meal; they learned to live so routinely with bombing that they developed an almost laconic indifference when telling later of their ordeals; 'pretty hectic' was the worst comment the author came across in reliving these times with those who had experienced them. The general rule was to drive on regardless of bombs falling on either side or the whine of approaching shells followed by a crash that shook the footplate under them. It is recalled how a driver or fireman who jumped down to use a lineside telephone to speak to a signalman escaped with his life, although he had been showered thickly with fine glass-dust from a bombed greenhouse; and how heavy storm-sheets were hung over a locomotive cab by the crew to shut off the glow from the firebox door which might make it a target from the air. The normal heat of the engine magnified in this manner on a sultry summer night was unbearable; 'like a bakehouse' was the

only printable description which came the writer's way.

Like the shining rails themselves, and in spite of the storm-sheeting on the cab, a steam engine could still give itself away by the luminous quality of its white smoke when caught in the moonlight, leading any prowling pilot to its cargo of vital freight.

However, comedy as well as destruction stalked the rails. We have the memory from one former railwayman of a repatriated corporal, returned to England from the Front smothered in oil and dirt. As he was himself a railwayman in civilian life, he knew at once where to obtain a bucket of water for washing, and was left to his own devices on the warm footplate. When an officer enquired after a missing corporal, the engine driver's retort was tersely accurate: 'There's one up on this footplate – but he's got no stripes on now!'

Engine crews learned to live with bombs as routine; almost casually, a fireman would clamber up onto the tender or the cab roof to kick off a small firebomb as if it were a pebble on a beach; to have poured water on this type of bomb would only have exploded it.

Sheer malice motivated some of the more daring enemy pilots in attacking non-military targets, including helpless lone civilians caught outdoors. We were told of a Dover railwayman spotted on top of a locomotive watering tank in the yards; instead of attacking the railway, the *Luftwaffe* deliberately shot the man off his perch from a low run over the railway, leaving eight children fatherless.

Crewing lines of potential bombs – a train loaded with ammunition or chemicals – was all in a day's work, especially when armaments were being stockpiled for the RAF's massed thousand-bomber raids on Germany. These railwaymen could not even take the simple shelter of the underside of a truck, when it was in itself a mobile bomb.

The blackout played its own tricks, ranging from the amusing to the gruesome. We have an illustration of this from a former driver who, on a night run, was warned by a signalman that a dead body by the track had been reported by another passing train; it was an eerie thing to look out for, until it proved to be a long fat cushion thrown from a carriage by a forerunner of today's railway vandal. Sometimes, however, the bodies were real ones, such as those of German sailors from a sunken vessel which were found by railway staff floating in close to the Locomotive Department sidings at Dover.

Home Guard

Railway branches of the LDV (Local Defence Volunteers, later to be renamed the Home Guard) were numerous, manned by staffs of stations and depots. By mid-1940 the Southern in Kent boasted nearly five thousand members, instructed in all manner of duties for relieving more skilled men; from working a stirrup pump to

Class N1 No. 31876 at the left of picture and Class H No. 31322 at the right, at Gillingham shed.

manning mobile guns, from fitness drill to capturing a stray parachutist and rescuing bomb victims. The Dover branch fought against the highest odds, being shelled as well as bombed, and thus earning their local nickname of the Hell Fire Corner Boys. Their wives often became involved, too, doling out endless cups of tea during exercises. They learned to anticipate emergencies on the line, in the same way that peace-time dwellers by the railway were sometimes subconsciously aware of possible disaster. The author's mother, for instance, always kept handy a large bag of old sheets and pillowcases cut into bandage lengths in case there was a crash near her lineside home.

By nightmare train into Kent

For civilians, travelling into Kent during air raids was a nightmarish experience. We cannot better the example passed on to the author from the 1940–1 period: 'I arrived at Euston station from Birmingham to discover that no public transport buses, taxis, etc. would take me to Victoria station, and the only Underground service only went as far as the Elephant & Castle. I caught this train after stepping over and round the hundreds of local inhabitants lying and sleeping on the Underground station platforms and subways. On reaching the Elephant & Castle I set off to walk to the Victoria mainline railway station with the noise of anti-aircraft gunfire, exploding bombs from enemy aircraft overhead, being sought by the probing searchlights. On reaching Victoria station I enquired if there would be a train to the Medway Towns that night (it was then 1 a.m.) and was informed that the only train in that direction would terminate at Swanley. This I thought would be better than staying at Victoria, so caught the blacked-out train on its hazardous journey to Swanley accompanied by the sound of the overhead bombers and defending gunfire. The train emptied at Swanley and I asked the stationmaster if there was a possibility of getting to the Medway Towns that night – he said no trains were scheduled and the best we could do was to go to the waiting room and catch the first train in the morning. About eight of us passengers, including three sailors, settled down in the waiting room but after a short time the stationmaster appeared and said that a six-carriage train was due to arrive from the Medway Towns and he saw no reason why it shouldn't be switched across to the down line and return to the Medway Towns. He said he had three boxes of fish to send, so while these were being loaded in the guard's van eight surprised and contented passengers entered one compartment of one of the six carriages and, after expressing thanks and appreciation to the stationmaster, set off for Chatham. Eight VIPs and three boxes of fish finally arrived at their destination, the three sailors to set off to HMS *Pembroke* to report "on time for duty" and not adrift, and the five civilians dispersed in various directions to reach their homes in the early hours of the

Two contrasting classes: 'Battle of Britain' about to pass a Q1 'Austerity' 0-6-0 standing at Faversham shed in 1952.

morning.' Thus reminisced John Chinery, one among many with such memories of travel in the bombing and the blackout.

The war drags on

Living in any railway town was a hazardous existence, comparable with life under the Dover shelling. Such major centres as Faversham frequently came under attack, as did the branches and sidings into Chatham Dockyard.

Strange assortments of motive power congregated at depots as every possible locomotive was pressed into service. Gillingham alone had about fifty on allocation, sharing local passenger working and heavy military freight; some ancient Stirling 4-4-0s with seven-foot driving wheels were seen, though completely unsuited to most local gradients, along with small P class tanks. Life by the line was thus a civilian's hell and a railway enthusiast's heaven, as stock from all over Britain came through on troop trains, such as rakes of LNER or LMS coaches pulled up out of the dockyard by an F1 or D1, with two P class tanks described as 'puffing frantically in the rear'.

And yet in 1941, in the very thick of the battle, the Southern was

105

able to introduce its most revolutionary-looking new locomotive, destined to set a trend which was continued in modified sister classes after the war: the air-smoothed Bulleid 'Merchant Navy' class, named after famous shipping lines. It was the sort of powerful Pacific that would have been ideal for boat trains had they then existed; but it was equally useful for transport of heavy loads of wartime freight.

As the years rolled by, Kent was ceaselessly bombed and battered. One of the enemy's most deeply penetrating bombs landed on Sydenham Hill, burrowed far down into the earth, and burst through the brick lining into the interior of Penge tunnel; and still Penge tunnel refused to satisfy its age-old critics by collapsing under a landslide.

Tragedy at Dover Priory

1944 brought destruction to Dover Priory station when one of the last shells of the war landed on the building, killing a number of civilians; but as usual the Southern soldiered on, thanks to the heroic labour of its men.

That year also saw some restoration of the ferry service, not on its former Continental passenger business but carrying hospital trains out of France, and taking in new locomotives for working Europe's devastated railways behind the front line.

Troop trains fell into two main categories after D-Day: those going down to the ports taking men towards the Front, and incoming specials known as 'leave trains', bringing others back for a brief respite. A smaller number of prisoner-of-war trains also ran, taking Italian and German POWs to hastily erected camps of wooden huts inside barbed-wire compounds, set up on parks, playgrounds and commons. As a small child, the author experienced being stranded on a remote country station at dusk with only her mother, one porter, one British officer, and a party of vicious-looking Italians for company; how thankfully we saw the train come in.

Finally D-Day and the battle for Normandy entered modern history: the Allied onslaught gathered a momentum that would not cease until the Nazi surrender of the following year.

The Second World War ended in 1945 with first VE (Victory in Europe) Day, and later in the year VJ (Victory in Japan) Day. Bruised, shelled and weary, the Southern Railway was still there, if not entirely in one piece, ready to rebuild its life and commerce; but not with its former staff intact for, according to a plaque later added to the Waterloo Station war memorial, no less than 626 of its employees died between 1939 and 1945. A large proportion of them came from the worst hit of the Southern's components, the former SECR territory of Kent.

8
Climax of Steam

With the coming of peace in 1945, the Southern Railway – tired and battered like the people and places it served – entered another era, one of both restoration of the old and turning to the new. The next decade's landmarks ranged from the railway nationalization of 1948 to the 1951 Festival of Britain; from the 1952 floods to the last great London smog of the same year.

Of purely railway interest was the early restoration of at least some of the old prestigious Continental services, as soon as there was potential custom to make them pay. For nearly six years the only cross-Channel connections had been military missions, and the sea coast itself had generally been out of bounds to civilians, thickly festooned with rusty barbed wire; forbidden sands apart, the Kent coast was in any case not the healthiest place to visit, especially the Dover area, facing as it did into the thick of the shelling and bombing.

Now, with VE Day and VJ Day already slipping into history, it was time to win back the day-to-day passenger traffic eastwards of the London commuter and Medway Towns conurbations, and to open up again the Continental trade which from early times had been the jam on the bread of commercial endeavour.

Briefly, railway staffs recall that trains trundled along the sea-front itself at Dover immediately after the war, on a short-lived offshoot of the harbour sidings; their function was to shuttle disused wartime metal for breaking up as scrap in the dockyard; it was customary for drivers too inexperienced for mainline working to be fobbed off with this monotonous duty.

West Country and Merchant Navy

Within the same year that peace was restored, the Southern introduced another of its latter-day unconventional locomotives, the handsome 'West Country' Pacific designed by Bulleid, which closely resembled his wartime 'Merchant Navy' class in its superimposed air-smoothed outer casing, sometimes described as streamlining. The 'West Country' class, visually combining power with elegance of outline, were named after Wessex towns and beauty spots because they were initially intended to serve there, though the class became familiar on the south-eastern section as well. Again, the system of numbering was indivi-

The *Golden Arrow* on the
former SER route to Dover,
here seen near Pluckley in 1959
behind rebuilt 'Merchant
Navy' class 35015 *Rotterdam
Lloyd*.

dualistic, ranging from 21C101 through to 21C148, following the 'Merchant Navy' class's numbering from 21C1 upwards.

Late in 1945, despite widespread devastation of almost every railway in Europe, a modified edition of the old *Simplon-Orient-Express* was restored, again with outward connections via the Kent ports. Not least among its operational difficulties was the existence of an Iron Curtain, which closed certain frontiers along the former route.

The Golden Arrow returns

Of greater everyday interest to Southern enthusiasts and travellers was the restoration in 1946 of the *Golden Arrow* boat train. Always the company's most prestigious train, it restarted on 15 April with a new feature which lent it even more distinction than the original train had possessed: the *Trianon* bar car, whose name became as familiar as those of the other First and Second Class Pullman cars. The new *Golden Arrow* was as spectacular a sight as the old one, still, of course, under steam. Through most of its post-war life it left from Number 8 platform at Victoria, which became known colloquially as 'the *Golden Arrow* platform'; over its gate a permanent arch was erected inscribed 'Golden Arrow/ Flèche d'Or'. Any engine allocated to this working was kept in top condition so that the famous train's reputation should never be tarnished. For many of its latter years it was almost exclusively hauled by *City of Wells* (34092 'West Country' class), noted for being kept in special trim for maintaining the train's tight running schedule.

The *Golden Arrow* was a proud sight, with her impressive smokebox plaque and slantwise arrow, the two six-foot-long arrows on *City of Wells*' sides, two more arrows on each elaborately crested Pullman car, and the Union Jack and French Tricolor flying from a special holder on her buffer bar. Lineside populations quickly resumed their old habit of gathering on bridges to see the train streak past with that unmistakable subdued sound of perfectly oiled Pullmans (quite unlike the note of any other coaching stock), with two baggage vans in Southern malachite green tap-dancing their own rhythm in the rear.

It is interesting now to look back at some of the Pullmans themselves, as well as the locomotive, recapturing the flavour of their names, some of which can now be seen on the new *Venice Simplon-Orient-Express*. Among them were *Zena* (*Golden Arrow* 1955-60), later transferred to the *Queen of Scots* and *Tees-Tyne Pullman* trains; *Phoenix*, formerly *Rainbow*, the car which was burned out in 1936 and rebuilt for the *Arrow* (she was also favoured as a special-train coach, often used by Queen Elizabeth – now the Queen Mother – and by heads of state including General de Gaulle); *Ibis*, a survivor of the pre-war *Golden Arrow*, which was requisitioned for war service and

110

'West Country' class 34091 *Weymouth* in original form, heading a Victoria train near Gillingham in 1958.

probably used as a mobile canteen car; *Cygnus*, the First Class parlour car, which stayed with the *Arrow* through most of its post-war life, and was also much used by royalty and other VIPs (briefly taken in 1965 to serve in Churchill's funeral train); and finally *Perseus*, newly built in 1951 as another First Class parlour car, which again ran in the Churchill special. The 1951 Pullmans (*Perseus*, *Cygnus* and *Minerva*) also went into railway history as part of a special rake of coaches constructed or restored for a unique Festival of Britain train.

Another variation on the Bulleid Pacific theme appeared in 1946. As the 'West Country' class was initially intended for service in Wessex, and therefore took West Country names, so the new class was designed with the south-east in mind. In view of the war which was so recently over, in which Kent – as Hell Fire Corner and the Battle of Britain county – played such a major part, this category was called the 'Battle of Britain' class, named after places and people associated with the war, or after squadrons of Manston, Biggin Hill and other local airfields. Numbered between 21C149 and 21C170, these engines included *Winston Churchill*, still working in preservation, *Biggin Hill*, *Manston* (recently acquired by a Ramsgate preservation society), *Fighter Command*, *Spitfire* and *Hurricane*.

Accidents at work during the last years of steam remained unusual, and even bizarre. The author has seen for herself the evidence of one former fireman's brush with the lining of Seven-oaks tunnel – a finger permanently imprinted under the skin with a wide black discoloration; grown-in remains of soot and coal dust which initially earned him six weeks off work.

Nationalization

In 1948 the independent history of the Southern ended with the nationalization of Britain's 'Big Four' railways into a single whole as British Railways. It ended a sequence which began with the

111

Class U 31806 at Gillingham in
1952.

union of the London Chatham & Dover with the South Eastern as the South Eastern & Chatham, and continued with the SECR's own loss of individual identity when merged into the Southern Railway in 1923.

Continental traffic recovers

A *Night Ferry* began about this time, composed of heavy French sleeping cars, usually with one or two former Southern day saloons attached at the rear for the use of early risers. These, however, generally ran empty, since arrival time in London was so early that passengers scarcely had time to dress as they were taken through the outer suburbs soon after dawn. Like the *Golden Arrow*, the *Night Ferry* kept its own sacrosanct departure platform, No. 1 at Victoria, above which was raised an illuminated sign reading 'Night Ferry, London–Paris–Brussels' under a bright crescent moon. No. 1, to many regular travellers into Victoria, was simply 'the *Night Ferry* platform'. As the *Ferry* came in so early, by about half past seven in the morning, the French sleeping cars with their pilot engine were usually still in at Platform 1 or 2 when the day's army of commuters arrived; they never ceased to be fascinated, on the way to mundane work, by this foreign train with its visions, through the windows, of regulation SNCF red blankets on the vacated bunks, and the rich midnight-blue carriage livery that belonged to the only set of European rolling-stock to be seen regularly in England.

A new heyday of Continental boat trains was under way. More daytime connections entered the timetable, usually with one or two Pullman cars in the middle as First Class accommodation; the rest was made up of ordinary saloons, for some time still in their distinctive former Southern shade (officially described as 'malachite green', which bordered on a bright emerald with just a tinge of toned-down yellow). Each carriage bore a long slim destination roof board lettered 'Continental Express Short Sea Route', and was hauled by one of the more powerful engine classes, including 'Schools', 'Lord Nelson', 'West Country' and 'Battle of Britain'. A *Short Sea Route*, as Southern residents called these trains, was impressive in its own right through its contrasts between Pullman brown-and-gold and ex-Southern green.

Coal, coal and more coal

Except in hotels and offices, central heating was still in its infancy in the 1950s, and the majority of homes still relied on coal fires. The coal lorry was as common a sight as the milk float, delivering several sacks to each house at little more than 7s 6d (37½p) a sack. Beyond the Southern Electric suburban area, most rail services also still ran on coal. Such sources as the Kent Coalfield at Snow-

No. 31904 on train out of Gillingham tunnel in May 1958. The goods yard with its bridge is behind the passenger train.

down were at the height of their production, and would remain so for another decade. Even today, coal trains are prominent among local freight movements; then, they were even more frequent, piled high with fuel, including such local varieties as Kent Nuts. Sidings were situated alongside main stations, and a few are still operational; one thinks of the large coal distribution centre at Beckenham Junction, where loaded trucks were nearly always to be seen standing in their network of sidings, awaiting transfer of their cargo by a system of conveyor belts into tall graduated holders, each containing a different size of coal. Many other coal yards have disappeared in the last decade with the almost universal domestic switch to central heating by oil and gas.

Until about ten years ago, many stations still kept their original stationmasters' houses, as part of the station buildings or standing just outside, when management was local and individual rather than exercised over a whole group of stations by one man. One recalls in this context the attractive old station house at Short-lands, with fig trees in its garden, which has vanished without trace to make way for a car park; the house was demolished in about 1965. Less favoured was (and still is) the exceptionally low adjacent railway bridge, on a busy main road, under which countless lorries have been wedged over the years, often remaining trapped for several hours with their roofs so firmly

115

'King Arthur' class 30794 *Sir Ector de Maris* seen between Gillingham and Chatham in 1958.

A now unrecognizable old-style Southern station with 31495 heading a local stopping train, probably only as far as Gillingham. Equally antiquated rolling stock is stored on the siding to the left. This photograph was probably taken shortly after the 1948 nationalization.

embedded in the arch as to cause considerable damage to the vehicle; the bridge itself usually emerges unscathed.

During the immediate post-war period, unless one were a favoured boat-train passenger, it was not usual to run straight through from London and suburbia to Dover in one unbroken sweep. Trains were earmarked in their entirety for Margate and Ramsgate, necessitating a change at Faversham onto a slow local train going on to Canterbury and the port. More modern electric trains for many years ran as one unit to Faversham, and were there divided with the front eight cars – two four-car electric multiple units – continuing to Ramsgate and the last four to Dover. This arrangement seemed inviolable until 1982, when new timetables

The French half of a *Continental Express Short Sea Route*, seen pulling out of Boulogne-Maritime station in 1957. It was common for a railwaymen to talk in front of a slow-moving engine through this crowded harbour area, blowing a whistle and waving a red flag in the old Victorian manner.

sent a train either to Ramsgate or to Dover but not both, though with immediate onward connections off all arrivals at Faversham.

Britain was still war-weary into the fifties, with Austerity dragging on together with a certain degree of rationing. The nation needed a lift, something to put the pride and the 'Great' back into Great Britain; and the centenary of the immortal Great Exhibition in 1851 at the Crystal Palace provided the perfect peg on which to hang a celebration of the country's achievements. The resulting Festival of Britain in 1951 transformed the squalid South Bank of the Thames into the showpiece of Europe, with massive pavilions tracing the course of every aspect of national life, from the Dome of Discovery to a television display, from The Lion and the Unicorn to The Natural Scene. Inevitably there was a transport pavilion, including a superb ground-floor display on the subject of railways; but of more general out-of-London interest was a special Festival of Britain Train, including the new 1951 Pullman car *Perseus*; other cars were restored for the celebratory *Golden Arrow* rake of Pullmans, among them *Cygnus* and *Minerva*.

Nature runs wild

If the Festival of Britain dominated 1951, it was baleful Mother Nature who ruled 1952, the year of fog, frost and flood. The bitterness of winter frost was backed up by the famous East Coast

119

An unrebuilt Bulleid Pacific stops at Sittingbourne. The Sheerness connection would have run from the platform on the right.

floods, which also affected the Thames Estuary and the Kent coast. Many lives were lost and incalculable damage was done. From the viewpoint of the Dover line via Faversham, interest centred on the former Canterbury & Whitstable Railway, where Nature proved that mankind does not always know best. Man had long since closed this branch except for freight; the line had scarcely been closed to goods as well when it was opened again, albeit temporarily, as the only means of bringing in supplies and materials for repairs as most of this line was embanked above water level. After several months, once its flood service was over, the line closed again, this time for good. Another major flood afflicted Kent in 1968, when much of the county disappeared under a flood which was probably unique in its sheer acreage – it marooned whole towns. The author's family will not forget the destruction of most of their ground floor by dirty water deep enough indoors to touch the piano keyboard. Inevitably BR's Southern Region suffered its problems, but at Shortlands the lesson of the great flood of the 1870s proved to have been well learned; though road after road lay under anything up to five feet of water, the embankment built after the previous flooding held good. Apart from fire engines and pumps, trains were almost alone in being able to move.

Rebuilding of Rochester signal box in about 1958.

The Great Smog

Reverting to 1952, we recall the Great Smog. The London area had been notorious for fogs ever since industry first went over to steam. Factories poured polluted smoke and chemicals into the air to hang there in still, cold weather until natural fog off the Thames blended them together into the impenetrable combination of grey smoke and white fog known as 'smog'. Steam trains contributed their own pollution – an argument in favour of wider electrification.

Smog was filthy to behold and filthy to inhale, with a stench that clung to everything and could be smelled even indoors, where it came down the chimneys. Its effect on the lungs was worse. It made it impossible to see more than five yards ahead, and brought traffic and trade to a halt. Trains ran hours late if they ran at all, as drivers were unable to see the old type of semaphore signal, whose red and green lights were too weak to pierce the murk. Quite unknown to modern generations was the fog detonator which was placed on the rails and set off by a train's wheels as they passed, thus acting as a guide to the driver. We who lived near the line knew there was a fog on a winter morning, without even looking outdoors, by the sharp popping of these detonators set off by the trains that did manage to get through. Compartments were almost as full of smog as the world outside, since it came in every time a door was opened.

On traffic islands and near station-yard entrances fog-lamps flared eerily. They were big black cans like kettles with extra-long thin spouts, out of which flames gushed with a sound like angry geese, identifying the location to floundering pedestrians. Otherwise a muffled silence prevailed, for little road traffic braved Nature's blackout. The worst smog of all came in 1952, when

121

Continental express *Short Sea Route* at Dover Marine. Pullman cars were for First Class passengers; others used ordinary Southern malachite green stock.

The *Golden Arrow*, in its latter days, waiting for passengers coming through Customs at Dover Marine. The station name has since been changed to Dover Western Docks.

'West Country' class 34092 *City of Wells*; the locomotive specifically reserved for working the prestigious *Golden Arrow* in its post war heyday.

chemists did a brisk trade in smog-masks; these were operating theatre type wads of gauze and cotton wool tied across the mouth, turning the population into a race of sterile-looking ghosts from some macabre hospital drama. In station waiting-rooms, choking passengers waited and waited, but miraculously many trains did crawl along, although timetables were a farce and the duration of a journey simply a guessing game.

Some drivers confessed themselves 'frightened to move', but the more adventurous braved the choking wraiths to grope and crawl a journey or two; 'they took their time' was the secret of getting through without accident, to the relief of those few passengers who had to travel.

Even the Houses of Parliament reeked of fog inside, a factor which doubtless influenced the passage of legislation ensuring that 1952 would be the year of the last smog as well as of the Great Smog. The Clean Air Acts ensured that such disruption would not happen again. From a railway viewpoint, the almost universal

'West Country' class 34005
Barnstaple heading a boat train
out of Folkestone in 1957. This
locomotive was also to be seen
on the more direct former
LCDR route to Dover in the
fifties.

Empty stock of the *Golden Arrow* double-headed out of Folkestone Harbour *en route* to Dover Marine in 1952. At this period the outward journey was to Folkestone, necessitating transfer of the empty train to Dover for the arrival of the inward ferry. The locomotives are former SER class R1 0-6-0Ts 31154 and 31069.

When winter was really winter. A country lane seen from a station entrance in rural Kent in the 1950s – but the trains got through.

change since then from semaphore to colour-light signalling was the final nail in the coffin of fog's power to disrupt the greatest city in the land.

Occasionally pre-radar sailings from Dover had to be suspended for several hours in thick land- or sea-fog, but cancellation of a boat train did not allow its crew an unexpected break; to earn their keep, they were set to clean out one or two locomotives at the sheds, one of the dirtiest and most disliked of all shed chores.

Cheap and cheerful

The Coronation in 1953 swept the last thoughts of war away, leading into a happy period of pleasure-travel at prices undreamed of today. There was reputed to be a milk train via Bromley South on which children could take a ticket at just 1s 6d ($7\frac{1}{2}$p) down to the sea, arriving at breakfast time. At more Christian hours, it was possible to pop down for only 7s 6d ($37\frac{1}{2}$p); off season it was common to go down 'just for the ride', through the Kentish orchards, with time for a quick brisk walk. Shop assistants could even pop down to Dover or Deal on their half-days, which did not start until one o'clock; again, so cheaply that it was practicable 'just for the ride'.

Throughout the fifties and sixties, the most noticeable features

128

of stations anywhere between Victoria, Bromley and the Medway Towns were the groups of uniformed sailors congregated with their kitbags on station platforms. Chatham station was nearly always full of men in naval uniform; men with the names of famous fighting ships on their cap ribbons, going on leave or returning to Chatham Dockyard. At Victoria it was not necessary to ask about the next train to Chatham; one simply followed the Navy to the right platform.

'Foreigners' bound for the coast poured through in summer, ranging from magnificently gleaming former GWR 'Kings' and 'Castles' on their own regional rolling stock, to Wakes Weeks specials bound for the fish-and-chips routine of Margate but following the Dover line most of the way, until they branched off at Faversham.

Trains every twenty minutes

In West Kent, electric trains ran at only twenty-minute intervals on the Sevenoaks line, and thence up the Catford Loop to London. All-night trains still existed to serve Fleet Street; it was impossible to be stranded after a late theatre show, knowing that at least one train an hour ran during the night from Blackfriars and Holborn Viaduct. Today, Holborn Viaduct closes after its last train leaves, at 7.20 in the evening.

This period was the climax of steam on the Southern, though a few diesel locomotives did appear, mainly on freight trains. The author vividly remembers, as a schoolgirl, being taken to London by her father to watch the departure of the *Flying Scotsman*, including a few brief moments on that hallowed footplate for a half-crown (12½p) tip to the driver. Before leaving we explored the station, and found in the darkest corner a queer oblong box on wheels, dead to the escape of steam, whose number is indelibly engraved on the mind: Number Ten-Thousand-and-One. That this seemingly lifeless rectangle could ever displace steam was as unimaginable as a cow in Battersea Dogs' Home. Yet steam's demise was nearer than we knew, for in June 1959 the first phase of Kent Coast electrification was completed, right through to Faversham, Sheerness, Canterbury and Dover. The *Thanet Belle*, *Continental Express Short Sea Route*, and *Golden Arrow* remained nobly steam-hauled, but more and more 'tin 'uns' (electric multiple units) crept onto the scene. Another half-dozen years remained until the end of steam in Kent; but the 1950s were to be its climax and swan song.

9
Living by the Line

Shriek followed shriek as the steam engine loomed nearer, while I lay helplessly in its path. I can picture now the firm black outline of its circular smokebox, and its small flowerpot-shaped chimney silhouetted against the deeper blackness of night. I screamed again. The bedroom door burst open and the light snapped on. My dealer of death was revealed as nothing but the shadow of a round hatbox on top of the wardrobe, with some small frippery perched on top which, in the light cast from a street lamp outside, had been realistically turned into the front of an engine, given an illusion of movement by the reflections of swaying bare branches in the lamplight.

Only a child brought up beside a main railway line would have turned a hatbox into a train, my first railway memory. In later life I came to bless trains instead of being afraid of them – they became a part of everyday life whose interest was infinite. To live by the line as a schoolgirl in the last days of steam was to realize how much the average spotter missed as he packed up his ABC book of numbers and went home at dusk; for he never saw the railway at night or in early morning when its interest was often greatest.

The gang at work

There were the troops of gangers whose work was then manual rather than mechanical, men who were attached to one area and whose names we knew, though their foreman was simply Flaggie, waving his red and green flags and shrilly blowing a whistle to warn his men of approaching trains. To local housewives, these men were individuals and friends, to be plied with cups of tea and biscuits over the wire fence as they did their work on the ballast in preparation for a night's track-laying.

Track-laying in the small hours could be seen only by house-holders whose rooms overlooked the line. Even if we could have slept through the din, many of us would not have tried to, for the spectacle was too absorbing to be missed. It was a far slower job than today's mainly mechanical track-laying, where the progress of the work can be seen before one's eyes; then, it was also rather noisier, with scores of men hammering and clubbing at old rails in groups, like a railway version of the 'Anvil Chorus', shouting 'Bill!' or 'Bert!' or 'Gimme that!' as if a road of sleeping residents

An impressive shot of a mobile crane in the act of lifting a discarded rail onto trucks on the adjoining line.

130

Gangers pausing during track work near Shortlands.

Class 33/2 No. 33205 on track-laying work. This narrower-bodied version of Southern Class 33 was built for the tight tunnels on the Hastings line, but is also seen between London and Dover.

did not exist. In the light of arc lamps and primitive hook-ups, men swarmed across the four tracks near Shortlands like black silhouetted demons, until twenty or more resolved themselves into organized groups leaning on their long levers in sixes or eights, waiting at the ready for their foreman's command: '. . . and *HEAVE*! . . . and *HEAVE*! . . . and *HEAVE*!' Several sweating groups bent their muscles as one man in a grotesque shadow-ballet of concerted effort. Nothing happened. '. . . and *HEAVE*!'–the recalcitrant rail budged a little. The crashing and clattering dragged on through the night hours as each length of rail and sleepers was laboriously removed and relaid, with two or three steam engines standing by with a brace of cranes, each adding its

131

A sign of cutback; buffet cars have been abolished from all Kent four-car sets; previously a buffet car was part of the electrical multiple unit.

An electric boat train shoots the signal gantry near Bromley on its way to the coast. It is identifiable as a boat train by the travel agents' labels on the windows.

own hiss of steam to the general cacophony; very different from the rumbling purr of a diesel locomotive today.

Next morning new gangs took over from the night men, as the final work went on, noisily raking ballast along the new wooden-sleepered track, singing and whistling to themselves as they moved, plied as usual by the neighbours with cups of tea. It was not uncommon for the first preliminaries to be done on Friday evening, and the last raking on Sunday afternoon. We lost a lot of

A semi-fast passenger train on the Dover line in 1955. The photograph shows the bulky but handsome lines of the tender.

sleep and cursed British Railways for all their works; but manual track-laying was actually something to remember for life. Today, sleepers are made of concrete, and the work is so mechanized that one night is enough for twice the old amount of work, and the ballast is chivvied into its final place by machinery.

Night time brought another spectacle which no longer exists today: the sight of engines being fired for their last laps into London. Through the blackness they rumbled, a satanic red glow from the opened firebox door reflected as a ruddy vapour on the underside of the smoke as it streamed backwards with the train's movement. Another moment, and this crimson trail was further

133

A post-electrification view of the *Golden Arrow*, with locomotive E5015 backing onto the train at Dover Marine.

A rebuilt Bulleid Pacific waiting at Waterloo; virtually all this class of locomotives also appeared south-east of London on the main line to Dover, usually hauling boat-trains.

The *Short Sea Route* express at Dover, with normal stock for ordinary passengers and two splendid Pullmans for First Class.

decorated with glittering sparks that flew like confetti at the Devil's wedding. This glowing trail moved into the distance, almost disembodied since the locomotive itself could barely be discerned in the dark. The reflection from its lighted carriages on our walls and ceilings faded away, and night closed in again until the next steam train passed.

Freight was (and is) a never-ending interest on this immensely busy route which copes with ever-increasing loads coming in through Dover from Europe; one of the few railway features which remain as enthralling under diesel power as under steam.

Rebuilt 'West Country' class 34017 heading an early-morning train at Gillingham in 1958.

Rebuilt 'West Country' class 34026 *Yes Tor* in the 1950s working through the cutting near Chatham.

Whatever its means of locomotion, a freight train shakes the house, and at night vibrates one's bed; its sheer heaviness gives a not unpleasant sensation as the vibration approaches, increases, and dies away again. This sense of weight was even more evident in the days of steam, before track was continuously welded, and the old-fashioned *te-rum-te-tum* rhythm of the rails gave its own emphasis to the general rumble. It was believed in the past that not every goods train was loaded, as it appeared to be, with tomatoes or tractors, meat or chemicals; for a certain exhibition in a famous London art gallery, it was held that several priceless paintings on

137

Freight and ferry; a characteristic scene in mist at Dover.

An electric boat train slowly
moving out of Dover Western
Docks. This photograph was
taken from the beach.

loan from Europe were inconspicuously brought in under guard
among crates of tomatoes. This kind of lineside story could as well
be true as imaginary.

Bucket chain brigade

New neighbours have no idea that older residents first got to know
one another by working side by side in bucket-chain teams, as was
common in the suburban parts of the route, where residential
roads backed onto the line. In reality steam equalled panic and
hard work instead of romance and, if one were especially unlucky,
the loss of a garden shed with all its contents. Throughout the

A modern main-line train on one of the oldest parts of the former LCDR route between Shortlands and St Mary Cray.

Overtaking on the bends near Shortlands. A diesel-hauled 'down' special on the Catford Loop pulls past a fast main-line train.

A dramatic view of a signal gantry on the Dover main line.

summer, embankment fires caused by sparks from passing steam engines were a constant threat, spreading rapidly alongside the track in the dry long grass. 'The bank's on fire again!' was the signal for wives to alert each other by banging on the dividing fences. Out they trooped, carrying buckets and basins of water. They would fling the water as far as possible over the wire fences at the bottoms of their gardens, where eager flames snapped dangerously close to end-of-garden sheds and garages. For every patch put out, the outermost flames licked towards two more, keeping us running in and out of our kitchens in a mad hurry. When at last the fire was out, our clean washing was covered with soot and smuts, and had to be rinsed out a second time and dried

The author has never forgotten seeing, as a schoolgirl, this 'foreigner on the line', GWR No. 7827 *Lydham Manor*, on the Southern. This photograph shows the engine in preservation at Paignton.

A four-car electric multiple unit, recently repainted from its former plain BR blue livery, seen here rounding the curves between Shortlands and Bromley South.

The very sharp dog-leg bend approaching Rochester Bridge. Here trains coast down from the heights of Sole Street.

142

Unlikely but true; a workman's hut inscribed 'Seaview
North Junction', temporarily
installed at Bromley South.

all over again. A brief lull; and then came an agitated alert: 'It's
started again!' and out trooped the neighbours for another dousing
session. By then the embankment was so wet that a further
outbreak was the next block's responsibility, and not ours. The
railway companies – Southern Railway and British Railways – did
their best by sending gangs of men with scythes to cut the long
embankment grass at regular intervals; but within a week it was
getting long again. This grass is rarely if ever cut now that steam is
gone, but the occasional flare-up from a cigarette-end flung from a
train window is not unknown.

Fire of a different variety enlivened our winters in the fifties and
sixties, as it still does today: blue-white fire from sparking electric
trains as their current-catching trailing shoes scraped a live rail
encrusted with frost. The effect before dawn on a January morning
was spectacular, when light as bright as forked lightning crackled
off the live rail and was further magnified by the glittering patterns
of frost solidified on the windows. The sound alone acted as an
alarm clock: a loud, sharp scraping and crackling of the metal
pickup shoe akin to the loudest amplified microphone noise
known to the pop-song world. Dazzling flashes shot off the train's
undercarriage as it laboured along, marking at intervals the gaps
between its three or more component units of four cars, each unit
having its own shoe system of electrical contact.

143

The *Golden Arrow* as most lineside residents remember her: with a 'West Country' locomotive, arrows on the sides and smokebox, the French Tricolor and British Union flags flying. In this picture the locomotive is No. 34091 *Weymouth*.

Last days of steam

Living with the railway as a part of life dulled the realization, halfway through the 1960s, that it was changing before our eyes, so commonplace a sight was a noble 'Lord Nelson' or a majestic 'Merchant Navy'. Somehow, the fact that 'steamers' were getting fewer and fewer did not register in our consciousness, even when a plume of smoke moving across the distance became the exception rather than the rule. The *Golden Arrow* went over to electric locomotive haulage; its coaches were no longer all golden, only the First Class Pullmans, and eventually it looked little different from a *Short Sea Route* to the casual eye. The age of the luxury train gave

way to universal road and air travel.

We still looked out for the *Golden Arrow*, though, as we did for the lesser *Thanet Belle* which (as its name implied) ran over the route shared by the Kent Coast and Dover trains as far as Faversham, where it ran on ahead to the Thanet holiday resorts. On its maiden run in 1948 the *Thanet Belle* had been hauled by the 'Battle of Britain' class locomotive *Manston*, named after the RAF airfield on the Isle of Thanet near Margate. The same year, this fine engine was given her title in a ceremony at Ramsgate station staged by the RAF. But the *Belle*, like so much that had seemed inviolable, was now doomed to die of modernity.

145

The open nature of the Medway estuary country; 'King Arthur' class 30796 passes the electric-train sidings of Gillingham in 1958. At this time Gillingham was the end of electric third-rail working – beyond here steam was still king.

Final electrification

On 12 June 1961 the other main route to Dover, the former SER line via Sevenoaks and Ashford, went over fully to electrification, together with lines from Maidstone East to Ramsgate via Canterbury West and from Maidstone to Paddock Wood. This completed total electrification within Kent, which had started as far back as the mid-1920s, and with it came the complete removal of steam power from this county.

In another six years the Waterloo–Southampton–Bournemouth route was finally electrified, bringing an end to the age of steam throughout the Southern Region. Except for special excursions behind diesel or diesel-electric locomotives, loco-hauled passenger travel had become a thing of the past. Probably this accounted for the proliferation in the sixties of camping coaches, advertised to holidaymakers. These were single saloons, including withdrawn Pullmans, shunted onto sidings in or near attractive resorts, and equipped inside with sleeping berths, kitchens and sitting rooms. They had the advantage over caravans of length and spaciousness, but the disadvantage of needing a ladder to reach the front door from track level, and the proximity of passing trains which disturbed those mortals who were unaccustomed to living with them.

It now remained only for the diesel age to write the last chapter of the story of the line from Victoria to Dover, bringing with it further losses of old institutions and yet, surprisingly, almost anachronistic revivals of the past.

10
Return to
the Orient

The 1970s and early 1980s formed a contradictory decade; a period of change and loss and yet of resurrection, which saw both the end of the *Golden Arrow* and the return of the English section of the *Orient-Express* in considerable glory, using some of the classic *Arrow* rolling stock.

End of the Golden Arrow

Through the late 1960s the *Golden Arrow* noticeably declined in appearance, as air travel from London to Paris took the edge off its formerly almost unbeatable timings. Steam haulage gave way to electric or diesel, and the Pullman cars were gradually reduced in number in favour of standard stock until only two or three were left in the middle of the train for use by the last generation of First Class passengers for whom flying lacked the magic of luxury train travel.

In the autumn of 1972 the *Golden Arrow* made its last run, including the Pullman cars *Cygnus*, *Perseus* and *Phoenix* in its rake. At journey's end one of the local drivers was detailed to take charge of the two famous buffer flags, guarding them against the attentions of souvenir-hunters – the Union Jack and the Tricolor which used to flutter so proudly under the smokebox arrow symbol. We who lived by the line watched it go, as if something less tangible than a train had gone out of our lives. By then the *Arrow* had served the Paris route for forty-three years, almost as much favoured by royalty, theatrical people and political VIPs as was the *Orient-Express*. Among BR's reasons for withdrawing the train was that the Pullmans had reached the end of their useful lives, short of extensive rebuilding; they would be replaced by an ordinary electric boat train without a name, running via Folkestone instead of Dover, whereas the *Golden Arrow* and its counterpart the *Flèche d'Or* had connected chiefly through the Dover–Calais crossing.

All that was left was a public house facing Dover Marine station approaches and named 'The Golden Arrow', painted in Southern malachite green with arrow emblems copied from the train; and also a much newer hostelry of the same name beside the bridge at Beckenham under which the train habitually ran, with the entire top section of an old semaphore signal gantry outside, the largest pub-sign in west Kent.

147

The splendour of the restored *Venice-Simplon-Orient-Express* rake of Pullman cars, here just clearing Shortlands on the Catford Loop side.

And yet history was still to take a couple of further twists. An invitation to see the *Golden Arrow* again many years after its withdrawal was one that the author could not decline, even though it meant travelling from Kent to Yorkshire before 11 am. The occasion was a special re-run and one-day reconstruction of the *Golden Arrow* behind its most frequently rostered locomotive of the last days, *City of Wells*, the noble 'West Country' Pacific which ended its great days as a rusting hulk in a Welsh scrapyard. No. 34092 was never rebuilt without Bulleid's distinctive outer casing, keeping her original outline even in abandonment. So poor was her outward condition that only true enthusiasts could visualize restoration to her old condition and to working order. However, ten years' painstaking work at the Keighley & Worth Valley Railway transformed the pathetic heap of old scrap into the *City of Wells* of memory; gleaming in green, quietly hissing steam, adorned with the once-familiar arrows.

This engine had been named originally by the Bishop of Bath and Wells; now she was renamed by the Mayor of Wells and the Lord Mayor of Bradford. Behind her stretched a train of assorted

148

What remained of Sheerness Station following an accident in 1970, when a train hit the buffers, slid off its bogies, demolished most of the station and careered into the forecourt.

KWVR stock, but including a couple of Pullmans and two authentic-looking Southern baggage-vans. The writer was lucky enough to be aboard the best of the Pullman cars, savouring again the atmosphere of an *Arrow* journey in the sheer elegance of polished brass, exquisite woodwork, deeply upholstered green velvet armchairs, spotless linen, and red-shaded brass table-lamps.

But even this was not quite the end of the line. At the spectacular pageant mounted by British Rail to commemorate the Rainhill Trials in 1980, a restored 'Merchant Navy' locomotive was dressed in *Golden Arrow* plaques and headboards and coupled to two of three preserved Pullmans to give the crowds some small idea how this once-magnificent train looked. Like King Charles, the *Golden Arrow* was proving to be 'an unconscionable time a-dying'.

By the late sixties, the *Continental Express Short Sea Route* no longer existed in name, though in practice it continued as one or more daily boat trains of ordinary electric multiple units running direct to Dover or Folkestone; a boat train like this is now identifiable as such only by the travel agents' labels stuck on the windows, for several companies' clients may share the same departure for onward connection with a chartered overnight couchette train into Europe, making in all an average 24-hour journey.

This photograph was only possible in the lightest six weeks of the year: the 'up' evening mail train hurtles into Shortlands at precisely 8.25 pm. It always consisted of just three coaches, headed by a Class 33 diesel locomotive dating from 1960-2, built specifically for Southern Region.

Rear view of a modern Dover express running fast from Victoria, on the sharp curve about half a mile short of Bromley.

Last nights of the Ferry

Longest lived of the named trains of Kent was the *Night Ferry*, which survived into the first year of the 1980s, still as the only SNCF rolling stock (apart from freight wagons) to be regularly seen here.

As an alarm clock the *Night Ferry* was as efficient as the *Arrow*, a once-daily sight by which lineside residents governed their departure for work in the mornings; if the *Night Ferry* had passed, time was running short. Almost exactly at 7.15 am it passed the author's garden. It sounded so different from any other train that one automatically looked up at the note of the approaching Class 73 diesel-electric engine, so silent compared with the purr of the heavier diesel. Three French luggage-vans followed, and a couple of BR saloons (almost invariably unused by passengers at this ungodly hour) brought up the rear; between them lumbered and rumbled the rake of European sleeping-cars with their ponderous sense of weight. Passengers were taking their first look at the outer London suburbs as their train drifted almost languidly past. With only a quarter of an hour between themselves and their journey's end, they could be seen pulling shirts over their heads and dragging down luggage, against a background of red SNCF blankets and couchette type bunk ladders.

The *Night Ferry* was always difficult to photograph because of the hours it kept. Only in high midsummer was there full light on its inward run (and that only at the London end of the route), and never on its outward run. To capture even a streak of light and shadow as it left London after 9.30 pm was not easy, when even in June light was failing by that time.

The writer can boast seeing both the first and last post-war runs of the *Night Ferry*, for according to a schoolgirl diary it was spotted on 14 December 1947 (its outward inaugural date) and she made a special point of witnessing its final return in early-morning mist in October 1980.

New replaces old

Soon afterwards, as some compensation for distinguished trains lost, the region acquired a new and novel alternative transport to the Continent, half aircraft and half boat: the Jetfoil (hydrofoil) service from Dover to Ostend, which reduced the normal crossing time from over $3\frac{1}{2}$ hours to only an hour and a half. It gives the heady sensation of a seaplane about to take off, or a fast run on a maritime motorway, as it rushes up to and overtakes conventional ferries. There is a special boat train – the Jetfoil does carry enough passengers to justify one -- and it has railway interest in that its departure lounge is a converted waiting room on Dover Western Docks (formerly Dover Marine) station, whence passengers transfer by special staircases and ramps to a dock beside the station wall.

151

The spirit of commercial Dover: freight and parcels shunting outside the Marine (Western Docks) station.

Parcels and freight being shunted on sidings at Dover Priory.

Even common electric rolling stock has undergone changes in recent years. Until about 1979/80 each standard four-car rake of coastal stock included an integral buffet car; now they are gone, disembowelled to provide extra seating. Some of these units have been completely refurbished inside for further service, with tinted windows, strip lighting, public-address systems from the guard's van, and new seating; 'the same only different' as is said in Kent.

Loss of the evening mail

Another loss, whose actual moment of passing went unnoticed and unrecorded, was the fast 'up' mail which cleared Bromley South at exactly 8.25 pm each night – another useful alarm clock of a train. Its speed alone singled it out for notice, as it and its locomotive shot like a bullet non-stop towards London. It was always of the same composition: one Class 33 or Class 73 Southern Region

152

Freight, freight, and more freight. All Europe sends goods through Dover, where these yards stand just behind the western beaches.

locomotive, and three standard loco-hauled mail vans. Again, this train could be filmed only in the longest summer evenings as it streaked into view and hurtled past with a noticeable wagging of its red tail-light.

The 'Unnon Train'

One thing does, however, remain inviolate, a train whose colloquial name is probably unknown to BR. It appears in no public timetable or spotters' ABC, yet is immediately recognizable to those who live by the line as the 'Onion Train'; or rather, in Kentish parlance, the 'Unnon Train'. It carries more than onions, though on occasion it can be made up of as many as twenty vegetable vans, through whose open vents sacks can be seen. This nightly freight train also carries all manner of fruit and vegetables, containers of chemicals and cement, cars from the Continent, tractors and farm machinery, frozen meat and other foods. The sheer variety of its complement alone makes it a train to watch for, behind its regulation Class 33 diesel headcoded 'BA'. Until recently it had a companion service, just over an hour later, which almost vanished from the scene after the rail strikes of early 1982.

In these freight trains, even more than in passenger stock, the passage of the years can be discerned through the changes in function and appearance of the units forming them. Coal from Snowdown apart, open wagons have become progressively fewer, whereas specialist wagons for cement and chemicals, refrigerated meat containers, and trains made up of privately sponsored wagons appertaining to large industrial companies are seen in ever-increasing numbers.

153

During the 1970s Southern Region introduced a type of train which ran successfully on the other regions, the Pleasureseeker special, opening up for day trippers, at bargain prices, parts of Britain which were normally accessible only for a weekend stay or longer. The special train's arrival at a suitable provincial rail-head city was carefully dovetailed with a fleet of chartered buses or coaches, thus allowing passengers to spend up to six or seven hours in a distant part of the country, to enjoy its high spots and still have time for personal exploration. Pleasureseekers (later renamed Merrymakers, in accordance with the other regions' policy) until recently started from the Dover or Ramsgate areas and by various routes picked up more passengers at stations up to Bromley South, Beckenham, Peckham Rye and Herne Hill; but in 1982, for economy reasons, the diesel-hauled specials started instead from Tonbridge, with normal electric connections to and from the coast. By initially organizing membership as a Pleasure-seeker Club and today by free mailing list, BR was able to sell a wide variety of these one-off special trips, during the first years for as little as £3. Although fares have naturally risen steeply, these trips still represent outstanding value for less than half the price of the same journey undertaken singly.

We remember joining trains on various occasions for long-distance destinations as diverse as the Cornish coast, the Isle of Wight, the Norfolk Broads, Cheddar Gorge, the Brecon Beacons, the Peak District, Blenheim Palace, Blackpool illuminations, and the Spalding Flower Parade. At the farthest geographical extremity from Kent, we have been to Snowdonia and back in one day, or even to the Lake District, with time for a cruise on Windermere or Derwentwater. Carried to the limit of practicability, Pleasureseeker passengers have travelled as far afield as Glasgow for a tour of the Trossachs, a two-hour cruise on Loch Lomond, and time to linger in the traditional time of gloaming on those famous shores, though this did entail an overnight return. It was not easy for other passengers waiting for suburban trains to accept that the station announcement: 'The train at Platform One is for Beckenham Junction, Herne Hill and Glasgow only' was stating the literal truth.

During the late 1970s Blackfriars station, one of the two London termini of the Catford Loop, was completely rebuilt (the other, Holborn Viaduct, having been renewed some years before), but something of the older mellow brick station was rescued for decorative incorporation into the upper concourse of the new building. This was the long list of places served during the heyday of Blackfriars as a Continental as well as a suburban departure point, cut into distinguished red sandstone panels built into the former façade. To read them is to realize, perhaps for the first time, that this was not always a minor commuter station serving

Where else in the British Isles can one see a bus destination-board reading 'Calais'? Special buses run from Dover Priory to connect with Townsend Thoresen, Sealink, P & O and Hoverspeed departures.

Sutton and Sevenoaks; for these names include the rich men's playgrounds of Edwardian Europe, among them St Petersburg, Wiesbaden, Vienna, Turin, Lucerne, Brindisi, Genoa and Milan.

Return of the Orient-Express

Thus the old faded away and yet left something of itself behind. In another sense the old returned in greater splendour than before, as recently as 1982: the *Orient-Express*.

Like the *Golden Arrow*, the *Orient-Express* declined during the 1960s and early 1970s as luxury train travel was displaced by flying; elegance gave way to man's eternal quest for speed, whatever pleasure he might lose thereby. Gradually the scope of the train lessened until it ended up as a few special coaches coupled to other trains out of the French ports.

In May 1977 it ran for the last time in its old guise, but in the spring of 1982 was renewed as two separate rakes of superb historic rolling stock, one on each side of the Channel, discreetly modernized in accordance with modern safety requirements.

We who watched the *Golden Arrow* run for the last time felt as if history had rolled back, as we waited for our first sight of the English portion of the new *Venice-Simplon-Orient-Express*, composed entirely of antique Pullman cars, many of them last seen with the *Arrow*. Since that time, we had not watched the distance for the first glimpse of a named train. A thin streak of white was suddenly seen on the horizon, on the high embankment into Shortlands; the movement of the pure white roofs of the Pullmans. A Class 73 Southern diesel-electric locomotive rounded the next bend, bringing into view the magnificent spectacle of seven golden Pullman cars, running with that unique soft sound that

155

Re-staging of the *Orient-Express* in 1930s style during the launching of the revived train in 1982.

A staged publicity shot of a
restored Wagons-Lits car of the
Venice-Simplon-Orient-Express.

recalls the mechanism of a 1920s model train. At the windows could be seen passengers dressed in 1920s fashion for this inaugural run, sitting at tables covered in snowy napery, decorated for this day with slim vases of pink and white carnations. The full rake – usually run in the same order – was *Minerva, Ibis, Phoenix, Cygnus, Perseus, Audrey* and *Zena*.

The restoration of these coaches at Carnforth married historic detail with modern techniques; it was the first time a full train of Pullman cars had been reconstructed. Each was stripped down, and the electrical and ventilation systems updated; superb panelling, marquetry, brass and mirrors were carefully removed for restoration. The fine old timbers were coated with fire-resistant paint, steam heating was replaced by electricity, safety glass was put into the picture-windows, and the brakes were modernized. So exactly was historical accuracy followed that the original bogie and underframe plans were consulted before each wheel and axle was tested for soundness. The result was a set of historic Pullman cars with up to half a century of renewed life in them, capable of running at ninety miles an hour.

Seen from the lineside, the baggage-vans are almost equally beautiful, gleaming in rich chocolate-brown with elaborate crests and lining-out. Initially only one was run, an ex-LNER van of 1944 whose more mundane duties had included carrier-pigeon transport, before working on the East Coast main line as a brake van, in which capacity it also served with the *Flying Scotsman*. During 1982 a second superbly decorated van was added. The train as a whole has also been tried for extra-prestigious day outings, at high cost, to such aristocratic destinations as Goodwood Races and tea at Leeds Castle. Its normal route, however, is usually via Folkestone rather than Dover, but it nevertheless takes the more northerly Dover line for about fifteen miles at the Londonward end, and also on its Leeds Castle outings.

The European section of the *Venice-Simplon-Orient-Express* also consists of fine restored rolling stock, no fewer than seventeen coaches including carriages for baggage and staff, restaurant, sleepers, and even a shop.

Manston

So long as the new-old *Venice-Simplon-Orient-Express* continues to run, the day of the named train will still be with us. The day of Southern steam is not over either, for one of the best of the Bulleid Pacifics is about to be restored at the time of writing. *Manston* ('Battle of Britain' Class 21C170) has been successfully acquired by the Manston Locomotive Preservation Society and, from rotting in the ignominy of Barry Scrapyard, returned to her old home territory for permanent display. Several years of ceaseless

Maid of Kent Pullman car from the *Thanet Belle*, discovered in retirement on the Ravenglass & Eskdale Railway in the Lake District, 1980.

fund-raising lie behind this essentially localized venture. *Manston* was built in 1948 and shedded mainly at Ramsgate depot during her working life, which makes her of special local interest in Thanet, the area in which is situated the famous RAF airfield after which she was named.

A little fragment of the named steam trains of Kent even exists as far away as the Lake District, where alongside the narrow-gauge Ravenglass & Eskdale Railway is kept the standard-gauge Pullman car *Maid of Kent* from the former *Thanet Belle*, which *Manston* sometimes worked. It is only in a semi-Pullman livery without the full ornamentation, as a restoration to full livery would be not only expensive but also a thankless undertaking in an area where salt sea air quickly causes good paintwork to deteriorate.

Plans were afoot for the private restoration of steam on the disused Gravesend West branch running off the main line near Farningham Road station, by a new preservation group, the North Downs Steam Railway. However, serious setbacks have not been resolved at the time of writing.

Thus, if we were asked to sum up the present state of nostalgia within the framework of the modernized Southern Region of British Rail, it could perhaps be put into one short expression: the past is dead – but long live the past in the present.

Index

Page number in *italic* type refer to illustrations

Key to stations shown

These are <u>present</u> station names

1. Beckenham Junction
2. Shortlands
3. Bromley South
4. Bickley
5. St Mary Cray
6. Swanley
7. Farningham Road
8. Longfield
9. Meopham
10. Sole Street
11. Rochester
12. Chatham
13. Gillingham
14. Rainham
15. Newington
16. Sittingbourne
17. Teynham
18. Faversham
19. Selling
20. Canterbury East
21. Bekesbourne
22. Adisham
23. Aylesham
24. Snowdown
25. Shepherds Well
26. Kearsney
27. Dover (Priory and Western Docks)

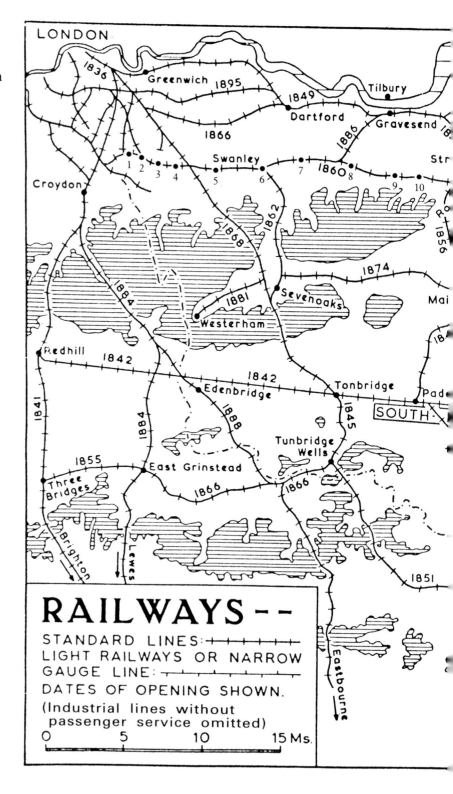

RAILWAYS --
STANDARD LINES:
LIGHT RAILWAYS OR NARROW GAUGE LINE:
DATES OF OPENING SHOWN.
(Industrial lines without passenger service omitted)
0   5   10   15 Ms.